THE WIND AT MY BACK

THE WIND AT MY BACK

A Cycling Life

PAUL MAUNDER

BLOOMSBURY SPORT
LONDON • OXFORD • NEW YORK • NEW DELHI • SYDNEY

BLOOMSBURY SPORT
Bloomsbury Publishing Plc
50 Bedford Square, London, WC1B 3DP, UK

BLOOMSBURY, BLOOMSBURY SPORT and the Diana logo are trademarks of Bloomsbury Publishing Plc

First published in Great Britain 2018

A catalogue record for this book is available from the British Library

Library of Congress Cataloguing-in-Publication data has been applied for

ISBN: HB: 9781472948137; eBook: 9781472948120

2 4 6 8 10 9 7 5 3 1

Typeset in Joanna MT Pro by Deanta Global Publishing Services, Chennai, India
Printed and bound by CPI Group (UK) Ltd, Croydon, CR0 4YY

MIX
Paper from responsible sources
FSC® C020471
FSC www.fsc.org

For my parents

Snow

A fox in the snow, as bemused as the rest of us. A London fox, lean and dirty, trotting down the middle of the deserted street, unafraid of a solitary human, moving from one pool of creamy street-light to the next, occasionally turning its head to check I was still following. A guardian-fox, escorting me home to my wife and baby daughter in their fug of roiling radiators and Christmas cooking. The ice encasing the pavement creaked beneath my boots – the only sound, for there were no cars on the roads and no other pedestrians. Usually the rumble and squeal of nearby trains would be audible, but in this great Arctic blast everything was muffled by the snow that fell daily then froze. Every morning we commuters pulled on hiking socks and boots and picked our way along the newly treacherous pavements, using for traction the freshest snow and an occasional patch of shattered ice. At the train station the staff shovelled salt onto the platform while we waited for trains that wore icicle beards. Cycling into central London was theoretically possible – the main roads were clear – but ill-advised. In the city the cyclist puts his trust in those around him, the bus and taxi drivers, lorry drivers, other cyclists. The combination of slushy roads and sleep-swaddled drivers with Christmas party hangovers eroded my trust in others just enough to leave the bike in the shed.

Throughout that December the temperature barely crept above zero, the snowfall was both regular and heavy. On the hills of the Peak District the snow was measured at 30 inches. From shivering tip to shivering toe, Britain was white. Life went on, of course, but it was slower and quieter. Postmen struggled to get to remote snowy villages to deliver Christmas cards bearing scenes of remote snowy villages.

The day after Boxing Day I loaded up the car with presents and all the paraphernalia a six-month-old baby commands, squeezed in my wife, daughter and mother-in-law, and set off on the long drive to Northumberland. In the boot I'd stowed a shovel, torch and blankets. Strapped onto the roof was my mountain bike. My mother-in-law, one of four sisters, moved to London when she was 21. She was following her heart, having fallen in love with a boy from Hackney she met on a beach in Spain. The other sisters stayed put, making my mother-in-law if not quite the black sheep of the family, then perhaps the romantic travelling sheep. And while she set about learning the strange ways of her adopted Cockney clan, her sisters got married, had children, but never strayed far from the family home in Hexham. Nestled on the lower slopes of the Tyne Valley, 20 miles to the west of Newcastle, Hexham is what the tourist brochures would probably call a bustling and picturesque market town. It is of course both more, and less, than that. There is an ancient, grand Abbey that still sits at the heart of the community's life. On the edge of town the houses are populated by wealthy executives who work in Newcastle but would rather not live there, and there is a thriving folk music scene. Yet there is also poverty and all its attendant problems – alcohol, gambling, drugs. The town may be pretty, with cobbled streets and granite houses, but this is still a post-industrial landscape. The leather manufacturers that were once the town's livelihood are gone, the tanneries with them, the wool factories have closed, as have the rope factories and the watermills on the River Tyne.

Above all, though, Hexham is defined by what surrounds it, the wilderness of Northumberland. Caught between the splendours of the Lake District, so closely observed and celebrated, and the more brassy pleasures of Newcastle, this quiet part of northern England is often overlooked. To the north of the town stretches Hadrian's Wall, beyond it the dark expanses of Kielder Forest. To the south, once the traveller has climbed out of the valley, the North Pennine Hills roll away towards an ever-disappearing horizon. Humans are sparse, livestock plentiful. The skies are huge and, as I was about to discover, unforgiving.

To the east and west of town the valley crosses the neck of Britain, running from Newcastle to Carlisle and carrying the River Tyne, a railway line and the A69. The latter is a spectacular and dangerously fast road, where motorbikers make their machines sing and, tragically often, disintegrate. Steadfast in the middle of all this wild open space, Hexham can feel like a staging post, somewhere warm and hospitable to shelter for the night.

That snowy Christmas we endured the long hours of faltering motorway traffic, staring mindlessly at blank fields and filthy cars, singing 'The Grand Old Duke of York' over and over to send our daughter to sleep, munching on turkey sandwiches. Our daughter, a plump pudding swaddled in a fleecy babygro, was the prize possession we wanted to show off to the northern contingent.

The next day was bright and clear. I packed a kitbag, heaved my mountain bike back onto the roof-rack and waved goodbye to my family. Already, after a single night spent in someone else's house, a sense of claustrophobia was starting to rub at my nerve endings, a sense that quickly receded as I drove out of town, climbing towards

Low Gate and Nubbock Fell, up onto the moors, a world of white on white, staccato black lines of fences and calligraphic trees, ravens striking out against the soft blue sky. On the more exposed slopes the snow had become sculpted into meringue-contoured drifts. By contrast the heaps of snow deposited at the roadside by snow-ploughs were lumpen and grey.

There were very few other cars on the road. After the frenetic jostle of London at Christmas, then the drudgery of the M1, this was a dazzling blast to my synapses. I passed through the village of Catton, its few festive lights the only sign of life, then dropped to the banks of the River East Allen, and into Allendale Town, where I parked and sat listening to the engine ticking away. The stillness was eerie. No people in sight, not even a bird crossing the sky, just thick cushions of snow on every roof, hedge and wall, even on the sturdy lower branches of a tree on what I assumed was the village green. A pair of park benches was almost entirely submerged, as if being sucked down into the earth. That should have told me something, but my brain didn't process the information – perhaps I was a bit frosty between the ears. I had a plan and I was going to stick to it.

Most cyclists will be familiar with the awkward knee-banging dance of trying to get changed into your kit inside a car. The key moment, if you are not already wearing cycling bottoms, is when you take off your underwear and try to wriggle into the unhelpfully clingy Lycra before your partial nakedness is noticed by a passer-by. On this day my preoccupation was more about the temperature than causing offence to the locals, who all seemed to still be in bed anyway, and I was soon zipped into several layers of thermal clothing. I checked my backpack for tools, extra clothing, a sealed bag of Quality Street chocolates, and the all-important Ordnance Survey map.

Buried at the bottom of the backpack, down with the crumbs of ancient flapjacks, nestled a compass, first-aid kit, bright orange whistle, and a small device for starting fires I'd brought home from a trip to the Arctic a few years before. I'd never come even remotely close to using any of these survival aids – I only really carried them because they boosted my sense of being a rugged outdoorsy type – but today, out on the moors in the snow, there seemed a fairly good reason to take them. After a quick check of the map I swung my leg over the saddle.

Riding on snow-covered roads isn't too hard given the right tyres. You quickly get a feel for this strangely pliable surface. Like riding on mud or gravel, your eyes scan the road four feet ahead of your front wheel, always assessing where traction can be bought and sold. Fresh powdery snow, older hard-packed snow, lethal stiff ridges that can send your wheel sliding inwards, friendly slush, traitorous slush turning to ice, invisible ice that covers the road like cling film. The joy of this ride was immediate and unusual: freezing air in my lungs, tyres crunching through snow, every part of my body – save my nose and eyes – swaddled in merino, polyester, Lycra, wool.

I pedalled out of town on a lane bordered on one side by a row of bungalows, on the other by fields falling back into the valley. As the dwellings came to an end there was a farm, deserted and motionless, then open country. The lane was narrow and its snow had been recently compacted by the weight of a tractor, the hieroglyphics of whose tyre treads could be felt through my own wheels. From the moor the wind came to meet me, energetic and eager to lick my face; the cyclist's best friend. On either side of the lane were snowdrifts, whiskered with green shoots and the odd looping bramble. Beyond the drifts were tumbled drystone walls. Ahead of me, I knew from the map, the paved lane would soon turn into a bridleway, which would curve across the hillside and up to Lough Hill. I knew I wouldn't get very far, but I did at least want to ride to a point high enough to give far-reaching views of this beautifully exposed land.

A five-bar farm gate marked the end of the lane. It was open, so I charged through, bracing myself for a change in surface and the extra effort required to push *through* snow rather than over it.

Cyclists often say that crashes happen in slow motion. My experience is that rather than one continuous action replay, the calamity is captured in several separate images, like stills from a film printed out on cards and held up one after the other. At least, this is how the trauma lives on in the memory. The sequence for this particular crash was both simple and utterly daft. First, my front wheel sank into a snowdrift so deep that only a slender crescent of tyre and rim remained visible. Second, the bike stopped. Third, I did not. A blunter shape than my bike, when I landed I avoided piercing the snow and ending up stuck headfirst in it with my legs waving about in the air. Naturally, given such a forgiving landing pad, I was unscathed, but I did resemble a mince pie given a hefty dusting of icing sugar.

Once I'd scrambled to my feet and brushed off most of the snow, I looked down at my parked bike. And then I laughed. What foolishness, what hubris. To think I could go for a jaunt across the moors in such conditions. What bloody arrogance. The bridleway ahead could be traced by the two drystone walls continuing to a vanishing point somewhere near the haze of land meeting sky. Between them an undisturbed eiderdown of snow. It could have been two feet deep, it could have been six feet deep; whatever its depth, it wasn't possible to ride a bike through it. This place, its wildest points, was closed to me.

I'd been hungry for open space, for the freedom with which this landscape rewards those who make the effort to explore it. I'd assumed my bicycle could take me anywhere, that the rules of the wild didn't apply to a cyclist in 21st-century Britain. As I looked out over the snow-covered hills, I realised that it was perfectly possible to die out there. Arrogance and stupidity, a splinter of bad luck, and I could have been stranded, freezing, beyond help, my pathetic orange whistle heard only by flocks of chaffinches.

I pulled my bike out of its impromptu parking slot, shook loose great chunks of snow and wheeled it back to the lane. The most memorable ride of the year had also been the shortest.

In 1967 a young artist called Richard Long, a student at Central Saint Martins, took a train out of London from Waterloo station. When the train reached open fields, Long got off at the next stop and walked to a nearby meadow. There he walked in a straight line, back and forth until the weight of his footsteps formed a visible line of downtrodden grass. He had made a line, a path with a beginning and an end, an imprint in the landscape. He took a photograph of his line and caught the next train back to London.

A Line Made by Walking was to become a seminal work, and Long was embarking on a lifetime of making art that speaks about our relationship with the natural landscape, with time and with space. Walking is central to his work. The very act of walking is often the work of art; what ends up on a gallery wall – usually a photograph or a list of words – is simply documentation. Sometimes he has created shapes in the landscape, using rocks or sand or wood. Sometimes his walk, his line, leaves no discernible trace. As his status and reputation grew, Long was able to travel further, to wilder places. *A Line Made by Walking* was an intervention in a landscape already greatly shaped by human activity but when Long created lines in the Sahara Desert, or the high plains of Bolivia, he was engaging with wilderness in the truest sense of the word – places untouched by men.

When I was a child, before cycling gripped me, my sense of the outdoors, and of wilderness in particular, came from family walking holidays to the Lake District, Scotland, Dartmoor. Often these holidays were with an organisation called Holiday Fellowship, or 'HF' as everyone referred to it, that owned several impressive mansions in scenic spots around the UK, and for a not inconsiderable price they would feed you handsomely and lead you on walks in the surrounding area.

My father, being good at both walking and talking, and always with an eye for an opportunity of a discounted holiday, became a leader, which meant that his lecturer's salary could stretch to a week's break at an HF house during the summer holidays. So from the age of six I found myself bumbling along at the back of a group of middle-aged walkers, watching the rise and fall of mud-caked boots, thick red socks, sturdy British calves and swinging rucksacks, listening to the conversation of doctors and teachers and lawyers, wondering when the next snack-stop would come, but above all, gazing at the landscape.

When you're six you are engaged in a continuous construction project; building the world in your mind. Most of the time your world is a small one – home and school, the streets where you live. These places are full of wonder, but the wonder is intimate, intricate and controlled by the adults in your life. A Lakeland fell, where the wind slices through your clothes, sheep dash through the bracken, rocks slip under your heel, and the crags above frown at your puny insignificance, is a very different place. You sense that even the grown-ups are not in charge here. Landscape of this scale bristles with drama and blows apart the cosy world of home. There is always something bigger, something you do not understand, a horizon that cannot be touched. I walked and I looked. I learned about topography, about the way the land folded, fluid and resilient. About the beauty of an exposed ridge and the transience of human feet crossing a moorland bog. When the footpath was muddy enough my diminutive boots might leave a print, but most of the time I skipped from rock to rock, light and fleet and traceless.

Sometimes, when I was older and stronger, I would push on ahead, dangling just in front of the group. Then my eyes did not gaze out over the land, but followed the footpath. I saw how human feet have worn paths into the land, the obstacles that paths tackle, and those they avoid. I learned about the mutability of a path; how it can proliferate, crumble, change. Of course we always stuck to the path. The British, blessed with a dense network of paths covering the countryside like capillaries, do not deviate from the path. They have no need.

Richard Long has spoken of being brought up in a walking family, of taking for granted the paths and bridleways that allowed him to explore Dartmoor as a young man. Much of his art has used existing paths, they have been the line drawings made by his feet. But he has also rebelled. In *A Ten Mile Walk England 1968*, he walked in a straight line across Exmoor, a revealingly difficult thing to do. The start and finish points had no particular significance, though the route did connect three ancient barrows before passing a line of standing stones. Anyone recreating Long's walk will have to cross open moorland, jump ditches, clamber over fences and drystone walls, and crash through the undergrowth of Cowley Wood, where the walk comes to a rather anticlimactic end. The imposition of a ruthlessly straight line onto a natural landscape reminds us that, for the most part, the way we travel fits to the contours of the land. We make progress by avoiding obstacles rather than tackling them. The art historian Dr James Fox took on Long's walk for a BBC documentary about landscape art, and at its completion seemed genuinely unsettled by the experience. It's a work that raises more questions than it answers, he said as he stood in Cowley Wood. Perhaps part of the reason his journey was so strange was that it lacked any kind of narrative. Wherever we travel, and by whichever means, our journeys have meaning, even if that meaning is only to buy a loaf of bread. We travel in loops, we journey, then return. *A Ten Mile Walk England* 1968 has no such logic. Its purpose, its story, is hidden from us.

The route of *A Ten Mile Walk England* 1968 is challenging on foot but probably impossible on a bicycle. And, to state the obvious, riding a bicycle is a very different act to walking. To ride a bike is to use technology, there is nothing ancient about it. It's a humble, humanistic technology that frees us, unlike motor cars, which have developed into baffling robots that apparently have opinions of their own and would much rather they drove themselves. Cycling is of our world because it's a technology that hasn't slipped out of our control. For all the space-age materials now being used, at heart it uses a few simple rules of mechanics. The bicycle rewards hard work; we understand and respect that. And it is seductive, tempting us to go further, faster, higher, to keep chasing the horizon.

Walking is limitless, as Long demonstrated. Walking is for true explorers, those seeking ground where few have trodden. Want to climb Everest? Want to go deep into places where people rarely go? Lace up your boots. Walking is for those who wish to leave civilisation behind, to lose themselves in the natural world. But this is, at best, an act of nostalgia. Long ago we lost a direct relationship with the wild. Creatures of technology, our lives have been immeasurably enhanced by the industrial age, and our relationship with the natural landscape has grown complex, fraught with all the love and insecurity a grown-up child feels for his parents.

Cycling is not better than walking, per se. Yet in the 21st century it is a better cipher for our relationship with landscape. Cycling is limited – as I discovered that Christmas in Northumberland – to another form of technology, roads. So cycling is always connected to civilisation. The cyclist has a dialogue with the landscape around him. And because landscape has an identity – cultural, social, political and economic – the cyclist is engaged with the world around him. Cycling may be an escape, but it is also an act of connection, sometimes in a radical and political way, sometimes in a sociable and benign way, and sometimes in a quasi-mystical way. For an artist this engagement is vital. I have been a writer since my mid-20s, and a cyclist a lot longer. These two cords run deep through me, and are inextricably intertwined.

Spring Stories

Walk through any park on a weekend and you're likely to see three- and four-year-old children zooming about on balance bikes. These dinky, nifty machines are scaled down children's bikes with no pedals and no drivetrain. The child simply scoots along with his or her feet, usually with head thrust forward and a determined expression. The name expresses what the bike teaches the child, specifically the balance required to keep a bike upright, that alchemy of movement that, as the saying goes, once learned is never forgotten. It's easy for balance bike graduates to adjust to pedal bikes because they've already mastered the basics of cycling; pedalling is the easy bit.

Balance bikes didn't exist in the late seventies, when I was infuriating my parents with my constant reliance on stabilisers. We lived at the end of a cul-de-sac on the edge of an Oxfordshire village called Watlington. Every day before school, I climbed onto my bike for a quick cycling lesson, and every day I droned up the centre of the road, leaning horribly to one side. When my father relieved my machine of its stabilisers I needed support, and that awkward stooping, something all fathers know and wince at, caused him such back pain that he improvised a stick with which to push me. An inspired idea because it gave me reassurance that he was in control, while removing his bodily support. I was riding unaided and he could nudge me back on course when I started to veer towards a parked car. Family legend has it that at first I mispronounced *stick*, calling out cheerfully, 'Daddy, Daddy, push me with your big dick!'

It was about this time that my father began cycling himself, taking the advice of a doctor, who told him that too much walking would be damaging to his dodgy knees. Once I'd mastered the basics of cycling, and grown more confident, I joined him on short rides. These first bike rides had a sense of discovery, made much more precious because the discovery was self-powered.

Watlington Hill forms part of a long curving ridge, enclosing the steep wooded Chiltern Valleys that stretch for 20 miles to the east. The village lies like a dozy guard dog at the foot of this picturesque rampart. To the west is the Vale of Oxford, the towns of Benson and Abingdon, and beyond is the city of dreaming spires, where I was born in the snowbound February of 1974, amid fuel shortages and the Three-Day Week. The early years of my childhood were defined by this landscape – the imposing hill on one side, the hazy, shifting Vale on the other.

We lived in a newly built house that my parents had bought from a drawing. Londoners who found their best selves in the space of open countryside, they were living in deepest Kent when my father secured a teaching job in High Wycombe.

Watlington was a strange mélange of a community. To someone cycling through, it would have appeared to be just another Oxfordshire village, with a quaint High Street, a homely butchers shop and a couple of half-decent pubs nestled among the cottages. Sitting in the centre of the junction of Shirburn Street and the High Street was the Town Hall, traffic elbowing around its red brick panels, often scraping, occasionally gouging it. Meetings of the Parish Council used to take place in the hall. On Saturday evenings dancing feet sprang off its ancient worm-riddled floorboards. And every Thursday in its open courtyard cabbages and pots of jam changed hands. It was the heart of the village – a little worn out perhaps, but inviting and benign. Around the village were strings of richly textured fields, mahogany polished by the autumn sun, swaying corn and barley in the summer wind.

Linger a little longer, though, and the visitor might have detected other angles to this place. The small estate where we lived was on the edge of town, facing out to the fields, and in its modern design had an air of the Low Countries or Scandinavia. It was populated by young families like ours, many of whom were new to the village. One of our neighbouring families was Swiss, and if this wasn't exotic enough, I learned that their first language was Romansh, an endangered tongue spoken by a tiny minority of Swiss. Quite how they ended up in this particular corner of Oxfordshire I had no idea, but their mother gave me doughnuts and told me, in a kindly but ever so patronising way, not to frown so much.

Our road was St Leonards Close, named for the Norman church whose graveyard our garden bordered. From my bedroom window I could see scattered headstones, wild flowers dotted in among barely controlled grass, a line of yew trees.

Opposite the church was a small industrial estate, next to it a gypsy encampment, this latter so permanent that I grew up rather confused about the meaning of the word gypsy. Elsewhere the poverty was hidden beneath the surface of a community that still had a sense of unity, of being a coherent whole. Even if the traditional rural economy was changing into something more diffuse, the institutions of an English village were robustly maintained, as was the social life based on school, church, pub. Despite being within 20 miles of both Reading and Oxford, it was a curiously isolated place. There was no railway, it was not on a road of any importance, and wasn't sufficiently pretty to be a tourist destination. Not that anyone particularly seemed to care. Huddled at the foot of the imposing line of hills, Watlington muddled along without the legions of London commuters that flooded the brick and flint villages nearer to Henley and Marlow. Those who discovered it prized Watlington's quiet community, its sense of enduring values and the beautiful landscape around it.

The actor Jeremy Irons bought a house there and could often be seen walking his dogs along nearby footpaths. A few years ago, as he awarded the prizes at a flower show, he told a local newspaper that he loved the 'scruffy village' that had adopted him.

Symbolic of the village's modesty is the anecdote behind its most distinctive feature – a triangle carved into the chalky earth of Watlington Hill, known simply as the White Mark. Some 270 feet long and 36 feet wide at its base, the triangle was created in 1764 on the instruction of local squire Edward Horne, who felt his view of St Leonards church, with its medieval square tower, was somewhat underwhelming. His solution was both ingenious and economical. Rather than build a spire, he had the White Mark cut into the hillside, aligned to the church tower, so that from his drawing-room window it appeared to be an impressive spire.

We often walked across the springy grass of Watlington Hill, peering into rabbit burrows, clambering along the trunks of fallen trees and in summer chasing the many varieties of butterfly that make a home among the juniper bushes. From the top of the hill we gazed out across the countryside. Oxford was barely visible on the horizon; more prominent were the twin landmarks of Didcot Power Station and Wittenham Clumps. Of the two I was much more interested in the Clumps, a circle of ancient beeches atop an otherwise bare hill. Later, I learned of ghost stories and folkloric associations, yet at first my preference was 80 per cent due to my parents' rhetoric that natural landmarks were attractive and power stations were blots. The other 20 per cent was due to the lovely name.

In winter, the cottages below the hill sent slow plumes of smoke into the air, while tractors ferried bales of hay from barn to field. When snow came, the White Mark vanished and became a sledging track. At the bottom you had to make a sharp stop or else plunge into a row of hawthorn bushes.

A lane ran up the hill towards the small hamlet of Christmas Common, so-named for the acres of land around it devoted to growing those doomed seasonal trees. At the top of the climb, just where the gradient slackened, a track led into a car park. Opposite this track was a farm – a farm with a secret. For if you knew where to look, and all the locals did, in among a flock of gently chewing sheep you could see a small concrete structure with a hatch door. This was a nuclear bunker, a human warren designed to shelter the great and the good of South Oxfordshire society in the event of atomic apocalypse. Put out of service in the seventies, it has remained untouched ever since, hidden though not terribly secret.

Those first short bike rides, beyond the end of our road, always followed the same route. We rode away from the village, along Pyrton Lane, with a dense wood of beech trees on our left, open fields on our right. Then turned on to Knightsbridge Lane, a medieval road that intersects the ancient Icknield Way, a mile to the east. This lane gently winds past Elizabethan Pyrton Manor, past Home Farm and New Farm, over a stream that connects with the landscaped grounds of nearby Shirburn Castle. It was here that the joy of cycling first broke into my bloodstream. The lane was flat, protected from the wind, and I could bowl along on my little red bike quite happily.

I soon learned that effortless cycling is momentary. If the cyclist is having a dialogue with the landscape, he never goes unchallenged for long. Knightsbridge Lane began to tilt upwards, my wheels glued themselves to the tarmac, and just as I began to wobble, I felt my father's hand plant itself firmly on my lower back. Together, side by side, we conquered Clare Hill. Not a high peak, but when we stopped at the top I felt that I'd ridden clear of the world I called home. I was free, facing out across Oxfordshire, the endless landscape in front of me, so open, so mysterious.

For a cyclist traversing the land, the horizon is always moving, a target that will never be caught. I was chasing the horizon then, and I still am now.

A change in aspect can be as much an upheaval as a long-distance relocation. When I was nine we moved from Watlington to Henley-on-Thames. And though only a distance of 10 miles, the world felt very different. Henley is in the same district of the same county as Watlington, its older houses are constructed of the same sharp flint, and in its many pubs the same Brakspear's ale is drunk. But Henley is a river town. It derives its identity, its fame, and much of its wealth, from the Thames. Its centre has a jumble of shops, pubs and cafés, and if you go for a stroll around town on a Sunday afternoon you will inevitably find yourself drawn to the riverside, where swans stalk the footpaths and motor launches dodge under the bridge, their owners looking rather too pleased with themselves. In Henley you can wear a straw boater and get away with it.

Come early in the morning, when the mist is still knitted over the water, and you will see rowers, eights and fours, surging through the dark water. A good crew is near-silent, their oars not only moving as one but slicing into the water with scalpel-precision. At the landing stage of the Leander Club, home to an embarrassment of Olympic gold medallists, the crews lower their delicate craft into the water, then clamber in themselves, impatient – I would imagine – to get moving and get warm. Rowers, of both sexes, tend towards the muscular balanced physiques of classical antiquity. When Henley Royal Regatta was on, the town was full of giants wearing Harvard and Oxford University sweatshirts, striding through the tiny streets with huge bottles of protein shake in their fists, sending us dishevelled hobbits scurrying back into our gloomy pub lounges, muttering about bloody out-of-towners.

While Watlington sits on the outside of the long curving shoulder of the Chiltern Hills, and has a corresponding air of being excluded, of facing outwards towards Oxford yet not close enough to lay claim to that dreamy city, Henley sits more comfortably in its valley, connected to the wider world by the river and a branch line railway. The industrial sprawl of Reading, unlovely but productive, is a short bus ride away, and by train you can be at Paddington station in an hour.

Transplanted from my cosy and familiar world, I was disoriented in this new place. The first thing I did, probably an attempt to latch onto something attractive, was to fall in love. She was the daughter of the woman who looked after my sister and I after school, and she was a full year older than me. The age gap was both thrilling and fortunate, for it gave me an excuse (to myself, no one else knew) for her lack of interest in me. Of course an 11-year-old girl wouldn't go out with a 10-year-old boy – the very idea was preposterous. In the woods behind her house I played on my own, building dens, dreaming up imaginary worlds, sitting cross-legged at the foot of a beech tree with a book in my lap. I was a quiet child, nearly to the point of catatonia, stricken with a shyness that made me a watcher and a daydreamer. At my new school I also felt the other children watching me, giggling about me. My new surroundings were excitingly awful; I wanted to be back in my cosy village, yet I liked the modernity of this new school, and the strangeness of having a river just down the hill. Eventually I made friends and assumed the position that served me well throughout my teenage years, and beyond, that of being part of a group but being the quiet one who sometimes did something funny or outrageous.

One Christmas I was given a racing bike, in gunmetal grey, with chrome toe clips and blue cloth handlebar tape. The following spring, when dusk's curtain was pushed back, I began to venture out on my own after school, happy to be alone, happy to be stating (again, only to myself) my difference from all those boys who spent their afternoons kicking a ball between parked cars or lying on the sofa watching Janet Ellis on *Blue Peter*. My earliest solo bike rides were a kind of running away. Nothing as pressing as an escape from bullying, more from a new and demanding social world. An opportunity to get away and look back. Space.

For a time my route was always the same, principally because my parents wanted to know where they should go searching, were I not to return, a six-mile loop we all referred to as the 'Bix circuit'. From my house I climbed out of Henley, alongside the fence of George Harrison's estate. My father used to joke that the former Beatle lived at the end of our street, which was technically true – his 62-acre estate, centred around a neo-gothic mansion with 120 rooms, did have its main entrance opposite the end of our thoroughly ordinary road. In later years some of my friends used to scale the fence and go exploring Harrison's grounds (which featured a scale model of Mont Blanc, built by its previous eccentric owner for reasons best known to himself) until the gardeners chased them out.

That initial climb was always a shock. The depth of effort required to get a bike moving on a hill, and sustaining that effort over a period of many minutes, was very different to the stop-start exertions of football or other childhood activities. Deprived of any opportunities to recover, the young cyclist has to learn how to measure an effort, and in turn this means learning to listen to one's body. That calibration becomes instinctive, yet holding back in the first 10 minutes of a ride, when all you want to do is blast away, is a perennial test of one's self-restraint.

Even at the remove of more than 30 years I can still see every one of those six miles. Over the brow of the hill the road bends between fields of rapeseed and barley, past a riding school (with its promise of girls in jodhpurs) and past the plastic lawns of a golf course. I'm wearing black wool shorts, perforated leather cycling shoes and a white cotton cap pulled down over my eyes. I tuck in, feeling my legs build a rhythm, absorbing the road vibrations through my wrists and elbows. Already I'm developing a sense of how to ride, for efficiency, for comfort, for appearances.

The road begins to descend and before I lose too much height I turn off on to a much smaller lane, single-track and always gravel-strewn, taking me into Lambridge Wood. From light to shade. The reassuring expanse of skies is replaced by a dense canopy of young beech leaves. Soft late afternoon sunlight glows through, illuminating the leaves' spidery veins, falling green-tinted into still air. The floor of the wood dips and rises in a series of mounds, burrows and hollows. When I was younger, maybe eight, I would have enjoyed running up and down those crazy slopes but now that I'm 10, I want only to swoop along the road that passes through, carrying speed from drop to rise. I glance sideways into the wood and see only darkness within. Keep pedalling, stay on the road, I'm not so grown-up that being caught alone in a dark wood doesn't scare me. If I puncture now, I'll ride it flat – to hell with ruining my wheels!

For the (rational) cyclist the woods are a refuge rather than a place of fear. They offer protection from climactic extremes – wind, rain, sun. If you're fighting a stiff wind across open moor, look for the valley forests, where your foe will be diffused. If the sun is making your head hurt, dive into the cool shade among the trees. The change in light, however, can be treacherous. One's eyes take a moment to adjust to the gloom – the inverse of the dazzling bloom of oncoming car headlights at night – and, deprived of clear sight, the fast-moving cyclist is briefly helpless.

Wrapped in the wood, the cyclist has less to fear than the walker who goes off into the undergrowth. A road may meander but it will emerge into the light. The sense is less of *venturing into* the wood, to discover something grizzly at its centre, than of *slicing through* the wood. Stay on the road and you will not get lost, and even if a nasty creature leaps out at you, odds are you can outsprint it.

So I keep pedalling, enjoying the silent, secretive movement of my body through the stillness. I have placed my faith in my bike. It has brought me freedom, independence, solitude. And I'm 10 years old now, no longer scared of the monsters – human or otherwise – who populate children's books.

When my younger sister started school my mother took a job as a librarian. Watlington Library was situated on the High Street in a quaint, slightly wonky building opposite the war memorial. Its two broad windows faced onto the street and it had one of those wood-and-glass shop doors that feel, when pushed, as if they are about to collapse, yet somehow never do. The type of door that cries out for a bell to be attached to it, though whether or not there was I cannot remember. It seems unlikely there were many book thieves in South Oxfordshire at that time. There were three rooms in the library, all with a polished grey stone floor that reminded me of a castle, and helped to make the library just as cold. Unlike a medieval knight, though, the librarians had a little kitchen out the back, with a grumpy boiler and a well-frequented tea-making station. Being the son of a librarian I was allowed to go back there and delve into the biscuit tin. It was surprising, yet pleasing, to see my mother in this professional and very public capacity. I was proud to be associated with the clunk-click of her stamping device. The date she printed on the frontispiece slip of your book was absolutely sacrosanct: the book had to be read and returned three weeks later or … well, the consequences were unthinkable.

One of the three rooms was reserved for children's books and there were four big wooden bins filled with picture books for the little ones to flick through. The more grown-up books were lined on shelves around the walls. Perhaps it was here, as I ran a finger along their tatty coloured spines, that my addiction to books – as physical things as well as homes for stories – took hold.

As I write this I am faced with a row of paperbacks that sit on my desk, raucously leaning against a pale blue wall. There are books on trees, books on falcons, books on tennis, birds, astronauts, rave flyers, New York lesbians and yes, some books on cycling. The selection is always slowly rotating based on whatever my current project is. These books have found their way onto my desk because they have some value to me, though the nature of that value is often veiled. Some – like the book on trees – simply contain useful information. Others have given me ideas about structure, narrative. And then there is a group of books whose role is to goad and reprimand me. For example, I am looking now at a Vintage Classic edition of *The Wapshot Chronicle* by John Cheever. It was Cheever's first novel, published when he was 46, though it is thought he started it 20 years earlier. This £8.99 paperback is a mass-market physical product yet it is also a work of art, and has no fewer than three functions for me. First, its unerringly elegant lucid prose acts as a goal, and simultaneously reminds me not to get too cocky – for no matter how good a paragraph I manage to turn out, it will never be as good as Cheever's. Connected to this is the exhortation Never Give Up; *The*

Wapshot Chronicle may have taken 20 years to write but who cares about that now? Works of art might explode onto the page, or warm slowly over many years. Last, I have a sense of Cheever as being my ultimate writer, a man dedicated to his craft, a man who felt himself to be a writer to his marrow.

I have another of his books, a Library of America hardback edition of his *Collected Stories and Other Writings*. Its cover has a picture of Cheever standing on a railway platform, presumably in one of the Connecticut suburbs he wrote about. Hands in pockets, wearing a heavy blazer and an oatmeal jumper, he gazes into the camera with an expression that seems to combine boredom, confrontation and bemusement. He looks ordinary and respectable but we know he is a remarkable man, an artist who has transformed his demons into a body of work that will endure long after his death. I like this concept of a writer as a kind of sleeping spy, embedded within a community but always looking at it with a detached, ice-cool eye.

To wrap all this up in one word, we may arrive at Inspiration, though that's a word that makes me anxious because it holds a curious position for me and, I believe, many other writers. I'm wary of what it implies, and what it says about my nature. What inspires you?, people ask a writer, to which the response is a sensation not unlike having your teeth filed down because they are too big for your mouth (something I myself experienced when I was 15).

Everything inspires me. Nothing inspires me. I don't fucking know.

Perhaps the question grates because ideas are so hard to pluck from the air, then so slippery to shape into anything resembling a narrative, that to connect writing to any single physical thing seems laughable. My dictionary, a heavyweight companion, defines inspiration as 'The prompting of the mind to exalted thoughts, to creative activity' and 'Undisclosed prompting from an influential source to express a particular viewpoint'. I like the word 'undisclosed' in the second definition. Despite the toxicity of the word for writers, inspiration does exist, at least for me, but most of the time its nature is not disclosed on a conscious level.

The layers of human activity, present deep in our landscape, the emotional resonance of past lives, act upon the writer's own subconscious layers. From these subterranean dialogues some image or phrase may bubble up into the fresh air of the present.

My desk is constructed from solid oak planks, braced at each end and held up by a sturdy frame. I've had it for 15 years and its grooves are stained by coffee, sugar, pencil sharpenings. The row of books and the solid oak desk is a mini-replica of the place where I first came to understand the relationship between books and writing.

In this place not only can you not deny that inspiration exists, you can't help but feel its presence in the very fibre of the building and the buzzing air within.

Totleigh Barton is a 16th-century cottage in Devon. Occupying a secluded position in rich farmland close to the River Torridge to the north of Dartmoor, to get there requires a stomach-churning trip down winding, ever-narrowing lanes. With its whitewashed walls and thatched roof, so soft are its edges that it seems an organic form, grown from the red Devon soil rather than built into it. Its former owner, poet Ted Hughes, donated the cottage to the Arvon Foundation in 1968 and ever since thousands of writers have felt their creative spirits cushioned and bolstered in its snug spaces. I went there in my mid-20s for a week-long fiction-writing course. My room was suitably spartan and adjoined another room that the staff referred to as the 'Poetry Library'. Lit by a south-facing window, this square room was lined with hundreds of volumes of poetry. In the centre was an ancient oak table, resting on an undulating floor of the same wood. Every morning I sat at that table alone and wrote – it was glorious.

Chill October sunlight streamed in and illuminated cobwebs in the window frame, the steam drifting from my mug of coffee, the page on which my pencil scratched out line after line. Around me were so many poems, enduring, written by poets long-dead, printed by publishers long-defunct. And rather than feeling intimidated – I was too naïve and over-confident for that – I felt these books carrying me along. The connection between the poetry and my own words was direct, dynamic. Whether or not my work was any good is immaterial. This was the very definition of an influential source prompting creative endeavour. I was inspired.

Such moments are rare and precious. Though fleeting, their legacy can last for decades. Mostly a writer has to depend on the more elusive and murky connections between place and mind described earlier. Am I now, at 43, unnerved when I ride through a dark forest?

Well, yes. I carry with me the stories of a lifetime. Myth, superstition, legend. Above all, fear. From Roald Dahl's wicked creations to the Wild Things on their island, I savoured fear and its defeat. In a quiet boy, is a lively imagination inevitable? Perhaps. Or perhaps it is better stated the other way round – a full imagination causes quietness because the mind is kept busy.

Certainly my mind was always chivvied by fear, by the growing sense of dark forces beyond my control. I see it in my own children, the incremental discovery of this thing called death. At first it is through a simple connection to Heaven, which exists up in the sky but may as well be Hampshire for the matter-of-fact way the children accept it. Then, with more stories, printed or otherwise, comes the discovery that death and fear are connected, and that danger doesn't only exist in books. At five, I used to demand that I go to bed with the lights on and the bedroom door open. Before closing my eyes I would get out of my bed to check there were no bombs underneath. I was scared of assassination attempts. A sign of an over-active ego as much as an over-active imagination. I was scared of the dark too – I'm still scared of the dark. But then I think every adult is. Anyone who claims they are not is lying.

Fear runs through fiction like a mineral through rock. I don't completely subscribe to the Manichean worldview that Graham Greene endorsed, but in stories at least the relationship between two opposing points is essential for creating conflict and emotional turbulence. Light and shade, love and hate, life and death. One holds the other in check, and in stories we can safely let more darkness cover us. When darkness takes over, fear can get out of control. An occasional conversation with friends goes something like this:

Friend: We were thinking of a camping weekend, if you fancy it?
Me: I don't do camping.
[Friend raises eyebrow]
Me: It's not that I'm being a diva, it's just that since *The Blair Witch Project*, I don't do camping.
[Friend laughs]
Me: I'm not joking.

The Blair Witch Project (1999) transformed the horror film genre with its Do-It-Yourself low-budget techniques and integration of narrative and marketing (when the filmmakers premiered the film at the Sundance Film Festival they launched a promotional campaign that listed the actors as missing or dead). Its story was simple – three film students travel into remote woodland to make a documentary about a fabled witch. After hearing of several unexplained violent deaths in the area, they set up camp in the woods, become disoriented and scared. The unseen witch – or something equally vicious – haunts them, prompts them to mentally break down, and ultimately takes their lives.

Here was wilderness as a site of malevolent spirits, somewhere that will drive you mad before you die. Its power came from our primeval fear of the dark, and our contemporary fear of wilderness.

When the UK was covered in woodland perhaps we felt it to be our natural habitat, but that era is long past. We feel at home with roads, shopping centres and roundabouts. The woods are dark and put us on edge. We know a tent and a flashlight won't protect us.

But back to Lambridge Wood, a spring evening, my 10-year-old self flying along on my gunmetal bike. Bursting out of the shade of the trees, under which little grows, and into the thin sunshine. At the hamlet of Bix I navigate a hasty path across the dual carriageway and disappear once more into narrow lanes flanked by large houses, paddocks, crumbling banks of earth salted with chalk. I descend into Lower Assendon, where an exuberant dog spots me through his garden fence and hurtles, barking, back and forth across the lawn. This is a useful fear – the sprint to get away from his fangs pushes my heart rate even higher.

Saturdays

Just as I made friends at my new school through playing football at lunchtime, so my father made friends through cycling. Men tend to connect through shared activity – we feel perhaps less guarded when we're engaged in sport, more vulnerable and therefore more open. And of course there is a common subject to discuss, something safely impersonal to cover up any anxiety about making a more meaningful connection. For me, making friends through shared activity was a good cover, because the focus was on the activity, not conversation. I was terrified of talking. To be precise, I was terrified of being required to talk to a group, to be entertaining and funny.

Later, in my teenage years, I started going to pubs – Henley is a pub town – and found them places of fascinating horror. Success in this arena meant telling stories, getting a laugh from your mates, often at someone else's expense, and flirting with girls. There were the heroes, whose social abilities only seemed to increase with the number of pints of Stella Artois they drank, and there were the watchers. Definitely in the second camp, I loved sitting and listening, sipping at my drink so slowly that it went flat (I would have preferred a Coke but this was patently not an option), just drunk enough to scrub off my anxiety about being picked on by one of the heroes of the bar. This has always been the position I've preferred: on the edge, looking in.

John Hutton was a good foil to my father. He was a lecturer, but at a private management college beside the Thames, whereas my father was a lecturer at a College of Further Education in shabby High Wycombe, having done his time teaching A-level Sociology. John lived in a large white detached house on Lambridge Wood Road (a cul-de-sac whose furthest reaches bordered the same wood I rode through on my Bix circuit), one of the poshest addresses in Henley. There was an air of respectable solidity to him. Affluent, though modest and without any trace of showing off, he was of a type of Englishman rooted in the traditions of cricket, the *Daily Telegraph* and public schools.

Most Saturday mornings he and my father would go for a ride and sometimes I'd tag along. They rode side by side, chatting, while I tucked in behind, sheltered from the wind, listening to their conversation and watching the miles slip by. John had something of the fifties cycle tourist about him. He rode a dark green bike, always clean and well-maintained. From his saddle hung an old but robust Carradice saddlebag of black canvas and leather. In winter he wore plus-fours with brightly coloured long socks and elegant leather shoes. On his hands were brown crochet mitts. He turned the pedals slowly and never got out of the saddle. When the gradient increased he went down through the gears onto one of the dinner-plate cogs on his block.

My father, in contrast, had a more erratic, highly strung style. Often his bike was making a mysterious noise, his handlebar tape coming undone and if he got too warm he'd take off a jumper and stuff it in the rack on the back of his bike. Over the following miles I would watch a sleeve slowly slip loose and dangle over the edge. He pedalled fast, for which he gained the respect of a racing cyclist like me, and talked equally fast, which I was well used to.

When the road tilted uphill, I took my prompt to swing out and sprint away. Out in front it was just me and those imaginary rivals who could just about desperately follow my wheel. Greg LeMond was still there, Bernard Hinault too, but my brutal acceleration had killed off Robert Millar and Charly Mottet. The commentary running through my head fragmented as the hill turned against me. Words were replaced by the roaring tide of my own breathing: pain obliterates thought. Then at the top, I reached down, flicked open my toe strap and my foot dropped, as if encased in concrete, to the ground. Bent over the handlebars, as I'd seen the professionals do, I sucked in great heaving lungfuls of air, then, recovered, I would start my watch and measure the gap I'd made on the two middle-aged men spinning tiny gears up the hill, still chatting away. They quite rightly chuckled at my foolishness.

On those Saturday rides we took in much longer loops than I was allowed to do on my own, up to 60 miles, and most were based around a café stop for tea and cake. Always we stuck to small lanes, where the traffic was minimal. Having cycled in the area for most of his adult life, John had a thorough knowledge of every road, lane, track and bridleway within a day's riding of Henley. I never saw a map consulted. For my father too these rides were lessons in the landscape, and over the years he grew as familiar as John with the network of bike-friendly ways.

For me there were other lessons. I listened to their conversation, which, as far as I can tell, they hardly moderated for my presence. Undoubtedly, looking back, they must have steered clear of any discussion about women, marriages, children, but I doubt this would have come easily to them anyway. I came to associate certain stretches of road with certain topics of conversation. The badly surfaced dip in the woods between Stoke Row and Ipsden was related to private versus state education (John was public school educated, my father left his comprehensive at 14); the exposed ribbon of tarmac over the Downs near Wallingford, where the sky was broader and the wind made the wire fences sing, was associated with a deconstruction of the Tory Party (John was a patriarchal Conservative, my father a former Communist who'd drifted very slightly to the Right).

There was a sense of gentle adventure to the routes we took. John seemed to delight in finding private estates with rights of way through them and gravel tracks that could be used to connect surfaced roads. For the most part it was a tranquil enough business, pedalling softly through the South Oxfordshire countryside, tuning in and out of grown-up male conversation, but there were moments that stuck in the mind. On a hot midsummer day we were rattling along a gravel track when my father called out, 'Nice hat,' then, 'Paul, don't look!'

On the grass verge a couple were having sex: he lying in the grass on his back, she astride him. Both were naked save for the cowboy hat she wore on her head. It all happened so quickly, and disappointingly, the memory has faded over time, but I can recall her spirited laugh at being caught, and that she made no attempt to cover up. Another life lesson.

When you are being led by another cyclist, you give yourself over to their guidance and the mind is freer.

The less you know of the terrain, the freer you are because you have no idea what is around the next turn. It could be a lightning-scarred tree, a watchful kestrel sitting on a branch, a cluster of parked cars, a couple having sex, or a village shop selling chocolate. You may be attempting to consciously think about something – to make up a story, or a daydream about the latest girl you've fallen for – but you cannot help but absorb and react to the passing world. Riding on small roads puts you physically closer to the roadside, without the distraction of cars.

Just as walkers follow footpaths, cyclists seek out small lanes. The British landscape is drawn with a multitude of these lines, so much so that they seem hardly like a modern imposition and more like a natural growth, a tarmac weed. Often a lane will feel firmly planted in the landscape, as permanent as the fields. Running through a holloway or between high hedgerows, the cyclist disappears into the land. Other times the lane may seem to skim the landscape, over moorland, and the shadows of low-flying birds flit along it. We love lanes because they bring us closer to nature, and because they remind us of older journeys, those of footpaths and tracks between villages. Riding along a lane, the cyclist brushes the lively habitat of hedge and verge; indeed, the humble hedge is the thing a British cyclist spends most of his time looking at. One becomes used to peering into its honeycomb holes, searching out small animals, berries, flowers and jettisoned biscuit wrappers.

At the age of 11, not yet lacerated by the insecurities of puberty, nor dulled by the mundanity of being an adult, the imagination runs unchecked. I wasn't half as interested in seeing small animals as I am now. I knew the hills concealed secret nuclear bunkers; far more exciting. What other mysteries could I stumble upon, if only I kept my eyes open? Perhaps I read too much *Famous Five* when I was younger. That cluster of parked cars could be a pack of middle-aged ramblers, or conspiring criminals, meeting in this remote place to dispose of a murdered associate. That tree might be blackened from a lightning strike, or from a wayward secret missile test. What would we do if we happened upon a briefcase full of £50 notes in the woods, abandoned in haste by fleeing gangsters?

On the rare occasions I vocalised such thoughts, my father and John didn't scoff or discourage me. It's an undiscussed feature of road cycling that it stimulates the imagination. And after all, one of the joys of having children is to indulge your own childish side.

As their friendship grew, so did their rides. As well as doing all-day rides far into deepest Oxfordshire, they managed to sneak in midweek rides on summer evenings, when the air in the Chiltern Valleys was cool and dusty and the light lasted long enough to afford a swift pint of Brakspears in Rotherfield Greys or Checkendon. And taking advantage of their teachers' long holidays they developed the ritual of going away for a few days on their bikes. The destination was always the same – Bromyard in Herefordshire, where John's brother-in-law owned a farm. By back roads, bridleways and canal towpaths the journey was 140 miles and they usually broke it by staying in a pub around halfway, although on one occasion when wind and legs were favourable they agreed to push on and do it all in one day, later regretting the decision when the Worcestershire hills began to roll towards them.

I was jealous of the escape these trips embodied. Not in the sense of escape from family duty, and work – I was too young to appreciate the need of adults to occasionally flee the people they love. My jealousy was about landscape, about the opportunity that these trips presented for my father to follow a meandering but broadly linear route across the belly of Middle England, towards a homely destination tucked behind the Malvern Hills. Despite his frequent testimony of block headwinds, punctures and incessant downpours, I imagined the pair of them pedalling easily through sun-dappled lanes, chatting away about cricket and stopping in thatched pubs for a ploughman's. For an 11-year-old I had quite an attachment to this kind of bucolic image of England

and its menfolk. I may have left the *Famous Five*, *Wind in the Willows* and *Danny, the Champion of the World* behind me, to be replaced by *The Dukes of Hazzard*, *The Fall Guy*, *CHiPs* and *Knight Rider*, but those books had left an indelible print upon my consciousness.

Incidentally, the American television shows left an almost equally indelible print; when in toy shops with my children I always gravitate towards the four-wheel drive remote control monster trucks and wish I were roaring up a backwoods Californian dirt road.

An important part of the imaginative appeal of these trips that I wasn't allowed to go on was that the route headed west. All through my childhood I associated heading west with romance and action. In *The South Country*, his prose hymn to the landscape and folk culture of southern England, Edward Thomas writes, 'Westward, for men of this island, lies the sea; westward are the great hills. In a mere map the west of Britain is fascinating. The great features of that map are the great promontories of Caernarvon, of Pembroke, of Gower, of Cornwall, jutting out into the western sea, like the features of a large grim face, such a face as is carved out on a ship's prow. These protruding features, even on a small-scale map, thrill the mind with a sense of purpose and spirit. They yearn, they peer out ever to the sea, as if using eyes and nostrils to savour the utmost scent of it, as if themselves calling back to the call of the waves. To the eyes of a child they stand for adventure.'

Our adventure started with my sister and I waking up to find ourselves curled in little cocoons made up of scratchy blankets and silky synthetic sleeping bags with cold metal zips, on the back seat of the car (a bright blue Lada), rumbling along the M4 as dawn eased into the sky. Ahead, we knew, lay Cornwall and two weeks of beach exploring, smuggler spotting and ice cream chasing. Western skies have always seemed to me more expansive, more welcoming. Holding in my mind the rugged stories of the Cornish coastline, as I grew older I got to know other layers of mystery – of King Arthur and Tintagel, of Avalon and Glastonbury Tor, of the Baskervilles in their besieged Dartmoor pile. I was convinced too that I would find love in this part of the country, that my dream wildling girl was hidden somewhere over the western horizon. In fact, she came from Kent, about as far east as you can go.

Conveniently, John Hutton had family in other scenic parts of the country. His elderly aunt lived in Suffolk and when he and my father planned a trip combining a visit to her with some cycling, I was invited.

There is a picture of me sitting astride a wooden fence. Behind me a beach stretches to a distant vanishing point, sky and sea merge in a blue haze. I'm wearing a yellow wool jersey, black wool shorts and a casquette perched on my head at a jaunty angle, and gazing out at the yachts and container ships sitting in the North Sea. In our few Suffolk days we explored the villages around Manningtree and Dedham Vale. This was Constable country, on blazing-hot days, the cow parsley nodding as we pedalled by, the breeze murmuring through oak tree branches. We watched, smiling, as car drivers hesitated before fords. Then we rode straight in and saw our spokes disappear into the river, hoping not to hit a submerged pothole. It was hot enough that our bikes were dry again within minutes. And looping through Wivenhoe, where the boats sat at drunken angles on mudflats, we came to the coastline, rode along reed-fringed roads that went nowhere other than the sea, screwed up our eyes at occasional clouds of sand whipped from the top of the dunes.

I was used to the Cornish coast, so this meeting of land and sea at the eastern edge of the country was confusing and intriguing. In Cornwall the coast has the drama of Atlantic waves crashing against granite cliffs, but it also has another reassuring rhythm. In every cove there is a beach accessed by a steep rocky path, or there is a fishing village. Explorers such as myself travelled by clifftop path and had the advantage of height – shall I descend here to search for smugglers or wait until an ice-cream van is visible? Height gives a sense of the wider landscape. But on the Suffolk coast there is no such rhythm and the traveller is down among the marshes, the inlets, the scruffy meadows and lonely clusters of cottages that have always lived with the knowledge that at any moment the sea may come to swamp them. The only height from which to gain a view is on top of a sand dune. Whereas in Cornwall the division of sea and land is clearly delineated, here the line is more blurred. The miles of inland creeks, channels and salt marsh mean that one can never entirely be sure where sea starts and land ends. The few low cliffs are unstable, visibly crumbling, acceding to the sea's relentless knock-knock. This is not a scary place yet the juxtaposition of idyllic farming country inland with the shifting coastline is unnerving.

Christmas with young children can be an exhausting business. Intensely enjoyable, but exhausting. A few years ago, on Christmas Day, I was so busy with present unwrapping, cooking, toy construction, washing-up, more cooking, eating, more present unwrapping, bedtime stories, more eating, that it was ten o'clock in the evening before I had a chance to relax on the sofa. By this point my wife and her parents were asleep.

As a little treat to myself I opened a box of bitter mint chocolates and sat down to watch a ghost story. The BBC that year had commissioned a season of films about M. R. James, the ghost story writer and academic. Mark Gatiss made a documentary about James and directed an adaptation of one of his stories. Earlier films of his stories were shown too, including the 1968 *Whistle and I'll Come to You*, Jonathan Miller's version of the 1904 short story, *Oh, Whistle and I'll Come to You, My Lad*. Miller's film, also made for a BBC Christmas slot, starred Michael Hordern as an ageing and arrogant professor who spends a few days on the windswept and crumbling East Anglian coast. Walking alone, he discovers that the erosion of the low cliffs has opened the land and made visible an ancient Knights Templar graveyard. He finds a whistle in a grave, and when he foolishly blows it, conjures a dark supernatural power that haunts him to the point of mental collapse.

Gatiss's contemporary version of James's *The Tractate Middoth*, the short film on television that Christmas evening of 2013, thrived on contrasting dark internal spaces with idyllic rural scenes. And though the claustrophobia of the old house that the story is centred upon gives the action a sense of foreboding, the supernatural darkness manifests itself in a pretty country lane in bright autumnal sunshine; an evil spirit emerges slowly from the hedgerow.

James, a medievalist scholar at the University of Cambridge, is now considered the master of the ghost story, and has come to be especially connected to that very English tradition, the Christmas ghost story. His stories carefully create an atmosphere of implied threat, often in what appear to be unremarkable places. The heroes are scholarly middle-aged men, reserved in nature, but curious. And a favoured storytelling device is the discovery of an antiquarian object, such as the whistle, that summons an evil force. Often this object is pulled from the land.

James was interested in the supernatural, religion and the limits of rational (i.e. academic) knowledge. He grew up in Great Livermere, Suffolk, and the region's landscape is deeply woven into his work. If, he seems to be saying, you have the temerity to pluck an ancient thing from this sacred land, do not be surprised if you unleash a terrifying menace.

For a more visceral and brutal kind of horror in the idyllic Suffolk fields and villages, there is the 1968 film *Witchfinder General*. Telling the story of Matthew Hopkins, a self-appointed witchfinder during the English Civil War, the film became notorious for its scenes of torture, rape and murder, made all the more intense for their juxtaposition against the sunny, pastoral Suffolk countryside. *Witchfinder General*, with its straightforward revenge plot, and no suggestion of the supernatural, is more akin to a Western than a horror film. Yet its power lies in its proximity to real events. While the plot is fiction, we know that Hopkins existed, and the seemingly benign English countryside was once the scene of horrific, barbarous acts. Time has folded generation upon generation. The physical evidence is long gone, but in the landscape a memory survives. One can almost imagine one of James's heroes coming upon a tree from which accused witches were hanged and summoning the vengeful ghost of Hopkins.

The English landscape is a place of horror and the uncanny. Scratch, or rather dig, at its surface and you may uncover secrets you wish had remained underground.

I knew none of this when, aged 11, I followed John and my father around Suffolk, daydreaming my way through the pastoral scenes. Too young to pick up on the darker nuances of the landscape, my imagination dwelt upon the layers of history, both visible and hidden, in the timber-framed cottages, village pubs, war memorials, pillboxes, streams, marshes and meadows. I saw Home Guard battalions patrolling beach roads, medieval battlefields strewn with bloody limbs, farmers guiding their horses as they pulled their ploughs. We stopped frequently at small ancient parish churches – they seemed to be a particular interest of John's. Having wheeled our bikes up the path to the door and leaned them unlocked against the wall, John would heave open the door and duck into the cool gloom of the empty church. Then, with our perforated leather cycling shoes tap-tapping on the stone floors, we would each set off on separate quiet inspections of the interior.

Writing this, I'm reminded of a documentary about Philip Larkin that includes black-and-white footage of the poet cycling up a churchyard path, hopping deftly from his bike and pushing open the door to the little church. In his poem 'Church Going', Larkin explores his uneasy relationship with religion. Trying with a laconic tone to pretend he doesn't care for religion, that its superstitions are outdated, Larkin instead displays a fascination and respect for the seriousness of religion, acknowledging its place in people's lives. His ambivalence is a reflection of a very English sensibility towards religion – an arm's-length respect. My principal thought, as I watched my father and John take their Larkinesque wander around the parish churches of this corner of Suffolk, was that the supernatural phenomena of the Church were just as bonkers as the ghost stories I was beginning to scare myself with. How could grown-ups believe in the *Holy* Ghost, but no other types?

These places impressed upon me the depth and richness of history that lives in the bones of our land, in the places we take for granted. I began to get a sense of the multitude of stories compressed into every square mile and the possibilities for books that created. I may have eschewed reading books for trashy American TV shows but that didn't matter – I'd begun to grip something much more important. That landscape shapes our lives, and our lives can be shaped into art.

Secrets

There is a stretch of road that I know so well, through sheer repetition of riding it, that its every curve is imprinted on my mind. It's a seven-mile route from Henley to Reading, taking quiet roads, and I'll always associate it with being cold. For a time, most Sunday mornings, my father and I would scoff down an early breakfast and set off for Reading. In winter, it was barely light and the untouched lanes were covered in a patina of frost. In summer, the promise of later heat still felt dishonest. Mist often slunk across the empty bunkers of Harpsden golf course. Our silent approach startled rabbits, foxes, deer, who had the tarmac to themselves for many hours.

From the Harpsden valley the lane hauls itself over a shoulder of low hillside, skirting beech woods, before dropping into the outer edges of Caversham, a prosperous suburb of Reading. Once, the day after the Great Storms of 1987, we took our usual route and found the road blocked by several fallen beech trees, wrenched from the ground by the 100mph winds. Seeing such huge trees lying prone, half of their branches crushed, their roots splayed in the air in an anarchic circle, gave the same sort of shameful shock as slowing down on a motorway to peruse a crash scene. In very British fashion, while absorbing this trauma to the landscape we took it in our stride, literally, for we picked our way through the leaf debris, slung our bikes over the dead wood bodies then clambered after them.

In Caversham, between Reading Rowing Club and a restaurant sitting on such a tiny island that for years I thought it was a floating boat-restaurant, is a bridge over the Thames. And at the centre of this unremarkable stone bridge the balustrade curves out from the pavement to create a semicircular platform from which the pedestrian can stop to watch the pleasure cruisers, scullsmen, eights and fours, the swans and the ducks. At least, that was possibly the architect's vision. The two platforms are too dirty, too pigeon-infested, and the road too busy to make them appealing for potential river-watchers.

The platform on the west side of the bridge, however, was our Sunday morning destination. This was the meeting point for the Reading branch of the CTC, the Cyclists' Touring Club. Founded in 1878, when independent travel on bicycles was first becoming possible, the CTC's original purpose was to find inns and hostels around Britain that welcomed cyclists. Ever since, the organisation has promoted cycling, defended cyclists' rights and, through its local groups, thousands of people have gained the confidence to explore the countryside around them.

In Reading every Sunday there were two or three different groups setting off from the bridge. Earliest was the long distance group, who typically did about 80 miles. Then there was a group who did 50 miles and last there was a 25-mile group, aimed at those new to cycling or lacking the confidence for longer rides. Every ride had a designated leader, every ride stopped at a pub for lunch.

If bike racing in Britain was a blue-collar sport throughout the 20th century, cycle touring was predominantly a middle-class activity. Every cyclist longs to escape into the countryside, yet whereas the racer simply wants an arena for his suffering and glory, the cycle tourist's imperative is to explore and observe. Conversation was wide-ranging and most definitely not about cycling. Much of it went over my head, the group were a brainy bunch. On some rides, my father calculated, because he values such things, there were more people with PhDs than not.

On longer rides, the group followed a well-rehearsed etiquette of riding two abreast, warning each other of potholes and other dangers, and observing the pace of the slowest rider. I often hung just off the back or off the front and when we hit a hill, I would launch into a lone sprint that I rationalised as extra training, but was of course just showing off.

Riding with Reading CTC opened up new places. Just by moving the start of the ride seven miles south, whole new landscapes became accessible. Like John Hutton, those leading the rides had memories like Ordnance Survey maps and the collective knowledge in any of the groups meant that every lane and decent pub within a 40-mile radius of Reading was known.

Heading east there were excursions to Burnham Beeches, the prosaic yet atmospheric expanse of forest wedged between Slough and Maidenhead, scene of Gordon Comstock's ill-fated bid to seduce Rosemary Waterlow in George Orwell's *Keep the Aspidistra Flying*. Often the rides in this area combined a loop through Windsor Great Park, prompting sarcastic salutes for Her Majesty from the left-wing contingent. The only ride I remember specifically was close to Christmas, a bright icy day, and on the way home we passed what someone claimed to be Billy Connolly's house. At the time the Scottish comedian, himself a keen cyclist, had his own primetime Saturday evening show on BBC1 and this brush with fame fascinated me. So much so that in the following days I went back later to that stretch of road and did interval training sessions on it, hoping to bump into the Big Yin and perhaps go for a spin with him myself.

The flat roads connecting the affluent villages and towns sprawling across the Thames Basin made for easy yet unsatisfying cycling. This was a landscape that felt neither urban nor rural. With its expensive pubs, roads full of executive cars and village shops converted into houses, it was a nowhere kind of place. The gigantic magnet of London held it tightly in place and sucked out all its identity. By contrast, even the London suburbs had a kind of anti-identity: they were the boring places that artists and musicians escaped from; the breeding ground for subversive elements like J. G. Ballard. Ridiculed and celebrated in equal measure by the generation of BBC sitcoms we watched on weekday evenings – *Terry and June*, *The Good Life*, repeats of *The Fall and Rise of Reginald Perrin* – the suburbs at least possessed the site of conflict between old and young, radical and reactionary. This place, however, outside the newly finished M25, had become a picturesque dumping ground for executives who wanted a big house and clean streets. It was eerie because it was mundane but also possessed an unnerving emptiness. During the week the commuters piled onto trains into town but even at weekends it seemed spiritually desolate. The men washing their cars, exhausted from a week in the city, frazzled by the daily grind. The churches held services for a handful of people who could remember when the village was a community. The pubs were full of tables of noisy braying families eating roast dinners while a line of locals sat at the bar in bitter silence. Little wonder Hammer horror films and *Tales of the Unexpected* 1970s television dramas were filmed in places such as this. The best horror films, the kind that affected me the most, were those that began somewhere mundane on a sunny day, and then introduced something uncanny, deteriorating into abject terror. The poor soul dragged into a labyrinth of pain and horror was usually an upstanding citizen in a suit. Whether an avaricious businessman or a righteous civil servant (obviously the only two types of men that existed in the seventies!), as soon as he let his libido conquer him, when a bewitchingly beautiful she-devil stopped him in Cookham High Street, he was doomed to an experience so horrific it would blow his mind.

Here was a terrifyingly camp inversion of Stanley Spencer's 1927 painting *The Resurrection, Cookham*. Spencer depicted family and friends emerging from the graves in Cookham churchyard, a resurrection scene of peace and joy. His work was deeply associated with Cookham, where he was born and lived for most of his life. Many of his works studied the people he lived alongside, celebrated their lives, and looked at how the sacred and the profane co-exist in English village life. By the late 20th century, if we are to go by television and film depictions of such places, we are much more uneasy about the countryside. Even if we dismiss horror films as fundamentally silly (and in many cases only filmed in Home Counties locations because it was cheapest to do so), there are innumerable murder mystery dramas set in pastoral locations.

It's easy to dismiss *Midsomer Murders* as cosy Sunday evening viewing, but the programme says a lot about our troubled modern relationship with the countryside. We like the way it looks, and the idea of life there, as long as that life involves endless summer days, exciting affairs of the heart and rather attractive police detectives. For most of us, a pastoral life like this isn't possible, so it's quite reassuring when someone gets brutally murdered – it gives us a reason to be thankful for living inside the ring road.

In contrast to Cookham and the surrounding area, the landscape to the west of Reading was more familiar and more reassuring, or so I thought. From Caversham Bridge we would usually follow the same route out of town, a line that sought to avoid busy roads, and in doing so was a lesson in miniature of modern urban Britain. With the group of cyclists settling itself into a comfortable formation we passed car dealerships, a casino, a leisure centre with its blue waterslides bursting out of its sides like intestines in trouble, the site for the Reading Festival and a nightclub, its car park strewn with the debris of the crowdspill that only happened a few hours earlier. Very few people around. Some runners, dog-walkers. At nine o'clock on a Sunday this place had no function. Its nowhere space is not open, and seems to propel us outwards.

Under the mainline Great Western railway and briefly onto the Oxford Road, with its Turkish kebab shops, Indian and Pakistani convenience stores and West Indian barbers. Henley wasn't so remote as to be completely homogenously white but this part of Reading, ethnically diverse and of low affluence, felt very different. Years later, as teenagers, my friends and I exchanged rumours about gang violence in this part of town, that drugs and prostitutes were available there, which generated entirely fictional bragging from some quarters. For us it held a fearful attraction because we were naïve small-town boys. But cycling through as an innocent 12-year-old, I am more worried about avoiding the smashed bottles in the gutter and the fast-food boxes blown across the road.

A long steady climb takes us out of the Victorian terraces and into mid-century suburbs. Instead of rusty fridges in front gardens there are clipped lawns and potted plants. White vans sit on driveways. Mustard-coloured lichen stretches along the low brick walls, marking out each castle's boundary. Like the houses back down the hill, curtains are pulled shut, and we slip by unseen. From such moments one begins to build the smugness of riding early through a sleeping town.

To the south-west of Reading is the M4, a brutal curving snake that channels noise and danger across the landscape. To the cyclist a motorway is an utterly alien world, an expression of the gulf between cars and bikes. Even going onto a motorway junction roundabout, via an A-road, can be terrifying. The cyclist knows this system has not been designed for them, that they are unwanted, unseen, unprotected. It's a question of scale: motorways and their slip roads and roundabouts are too broad, too open – they give cars the freedom to veer from side to side at will. As a machine for moving cars around, the motorway works perfectly, as long as everyone follows the same game of flow, with all its nuances. The human form, slow, small and vulnerable, has no place here.

Beyond the M4 lie the quiet rural lanes that will lead us away into the countryside, but how to get over there without having to tackle the horrors of Junction 11? Here, we encounter a form of magic only a cyclist knows. Where town meets country there are roads that could be described as happy anomalies: they seem to exist only because of some quirk in access rights, or because their presence has been missed by the commercial forces that plan urban expansions. Whatever the reason for their survival, these lanes are made impassable to traffic – to avoid the dreaded rat-run – and become the realm of cyclists.

At the edge of Tilehurst you can look down upon the M4 and its borderlands of retail parks and light industrial units and feel there is no way out of this modern horror, yet if you know the right road you will find Pincents Lane disappearing into the woods. Its surface pitted and dim from the untrimmed trees overhead, it drops sharply past a few meadows and some dilapidated farm buildings – probably the reason for its continued existence. For a minute or so you are shielded from the noise of the motorway and the teasing scent of woodland fills your nostrils. This closed road – not failed, nor bypassed, just closed because it no longer fits the world – can unlock a path through this world made for cars. Rain has washed mud and grit onto the tarmac and without cars to push it aside it has formed dark rivers down one side of the road. We descend with our fingers on the brakes, focused on the bike ahead and the dirt under our wheels. At the bottom of the hill, where the trees give way to exploding bright light, there are concrete barricades across the road with just enough room either side to swing a bike through. We have arrived in the car park of a DIY retail unit. From ancient woodland gloom to fluorescent motorised capitalism in less than half a mile. With wry smiles we coast down to the car park entrance, to the bemusement of those driving in, and ride the short distance to our next secret portal – a footbridge over the motorway. In single file, slowly, we float through mid-air, the destructive power of six lanes of traffic below us, and when we descend the long curving ramp, we are delivered, free to ride.

Other east-to-west lines converge here. There is the Great Western railway. There is the A4, once the primary route from London to Bath, and still referred to as the Bath Road by those in the cycling community old enough to remember the days of 25-mile time trials early on Sunday mornings. Now the road is still busy but the journeys are local and any trace of those glory days of motoring, when families in their British-built cars followed AA maps and stopped for tea at service stations for a smiling attendant to do the filling…

Cliché alert! Perhaps roads bring out the nostalgic stereotypes in us, or just in me.

Bumbling alongside the A4 is the River Kennet, a tributary of the Thames that springs from the ground near Avebury in Wiltshire. The Kennet forms part of the Kennet & Avon Canal, which runs from Bristol to Reading, but, confusingly, mainly follows rivers. From Bristol to Bath it travels along the River Avon, then there's a section of canal before it joins the Kennet and then finally, the Thames. Industry has drawn these pencil lines into the landscape of the Thames Valley, periodically rubbing them out and drawing a fatter, straighter, faster line nearby. First, canal, then train, road and motorway. Since the late eighties, economic growth in this area has been pushed by high-tech companies, whose bland and clean offices proliferate the borderlands alongside the M4, like a crystalline growth. Many of these high-tech companies are now multinational, billion-dollar concerns, but the origins of Britain's answer to Silicon Valley lie in a place altogether more secretive, somewhere with enough destructive power to wipe humanity from a large portion of the planet.

Ride south, leave the M4 behind you, and soon you enter a bewildering maze of man-made gravel lakes, channels and streams. So watery is this landscape, especially after being suspended in mid-air on the footbridge, that the cyclist might be forgiven for thinking getting out of Reading constitutes a trial by the elements. The road we take to cross this strange landscape runs along a culvert. Little dead-end tracks disappear off into the delicate-looking poplar trees that surround the water and further add to the sense of disorientation. Through the trees we glimpse a sailing club and the many lonely parked cars and khaki tents of that most solitary of creatures, the fisherman. A scattering of houses also hide among the trees.

For a while, during her most reclusive years, the English singer-songwriter Kate Bush lived in a house here. When I first heard this I was surprised. The lakes are neither beautiful nor dramatic; no Heathcliff will come wading out of their waters. It seemed odd. But no artist is exactly their work. Kate Bush is another product of the suburbs – she comes from the same part of South London where I live now, and here among the gravel pits, the poplar trees and swathes of blackthorn and hawthorn scrub, perhaps she found a house where she could get the privacy and the peace she needed.

The ground rises a little, taking our group into more reassuring territory – arable fields, dense hedgerows, an undulating lane. Hiding in plain sight is a theme of this landscape. Follow the lane uphill and you will notice that a tall mesh fence topped with a roll of razor wire has appeared just beyond the grass verge. The road widens and has an impeccable surface. Discreet yet assertive signs punctuate the security fence, forbidding the taking of photographs or sketching. You begin to get the sense you are being watched; that if you did stop and take a photograph, an unmarked car full of discreet yet assertive men would come and meet you shortly after. Not that there's anything worth snapping beyond the fence – a jumble of concrete buildings, industrial pipes, internal roads and some grass-topped bunkers. Yet when you know what's inside, you want to press your nose to the wire mesh and peer in.

The first time I cycled in this area I was completely unprepared for what I was about to witness. It was one of those dark February days when the clouds tumble over each other, growing a deeper grey with each passing hour, and you can never quite shake the chill from your bones. Our Sunday morning CTC group had headed out through Pangbourne and across the hills near Cold Ash and Bucklebury, turned south and were now climbing a gradual slope out of Newbury. In an effort to warm up, I was applying some pressure to the pedals and had drawn 50 yards clear of the others. The road was wide and well made, oddly so. Beside it was a deep verge, and from it, stretching her arms and yawning as if just getting out of bed, a woman emerged. Her tent was almost submerged in the undergrowth but as I rode on, more and more tents were visible.

Greenpeace and CND flags were draped over canvas or fluttered on makeshift poles. Among the tents, old buses and campervans were parked. A campfire sent up a soft pall of smoke, around it a group of women stood talking and drinking tea. So this was the radical and dangerous Greenham Common Women's Peace Camp I'd seen on the BBC News. Against the backdrop of tame, well-ordered, at times prissy Berkshire, the camp did have a wild tinge, but its only true threat was aesthetic. It was messy and colourful and most of all, it wasn't supposed to be there. Britain is not a wild place: every inch of the country is planned, owned and, to some degree, designed. So when a group with a shared political goal – nuclear disarmament – that runs against prevailing public opinion park up outside an American airbase, it becomes a national scandal. Despite the best efforts of the government, the police and the right-wing media, the Women's Camp lasted 19 years. The Americans pulled out their missiles in 1991, because of strategic changes rather than because of the protests, but the camp remained in situ until 2000. Soon after, Greenham Common was redeveloped. Today you will find a business park and common parkland, but the ghosts of Cold War conflict still linger.

Absorbed by the spectacle of the camp, I must have slowed down, for I found the rest of the group were on my wheel. One of the men suggested I test my sprinting ability by shouting 'Go home and do the washing-up' just to see what happened.

After the Greenham Camp dissolved the focus of nuclear protest shifted a mile down the road to neighbouring Aldermaston, home to the Atomic Weapons Establishment (AWE). But here the protests never quite achieved the spectacular Mexican stand-off that happened at Greenham. The authorities had learned their lessons about moving protesters on before they get a chance to settle, and on a practical level there wasn't much common space on which to camp. On a psychological level too, protests against AWE were more muted, more complex. Greenham was a clear concept – British women against nuclear weapons, as embodied by American Cold War aggression. The camp captured the imagination because it became an emblem for feminism. And the British love an underdog. Once the Yanks were out, the Cold War over, the argument – that we should disarm – didn't fundamentally change, but the target was broader, harder to pin down. Nuclear disarmament was still the goal but after the Cold War, what was the focus? Who was the enemy?

In the eighties the Greenham protesters joined hands to stop lorries bearing huge American missiles as they entered and left the base. AWE gave the protesters no such media-friendly image. It looked – still does – like a campus of shabby, outdated industrial buildings. Only its name gives any indication of what goes on inside. There is never anything as vulgar as a missile on display. Opposite its front gate is a modern housing estate. Everyday life continues outside the razor wire – banal, humdrum, blithely accepting of the weapons factory over the road. There has been a nuclear weapons establishment on the site since 1955. Everyone living nearby has chosen to do so. Are they afraid? It would appear not. Though perhaps they should be.

Ever since that wintry day in the eighties when I first saw, and understood, the Greenham Common Women's Peace Camp, the nuclear sites at Aldermaston and nearby Burghfield have lodged themselves deep in my imagination. They are dark matter, powerful and terrifying. Part of their power lies in the secrecy around them. These are places that hide in plain sight, but when you look at them you are encouraged to avert your eyes. The further you go into the Atomic Weapons Establishment, the more secret it gets, and the more dangerous. I still can't quite get over the fact of these bomb factories existing cheek by jowl with normal, boring Berkshire villages. If they were concealed in deep caves in the Scottish Highlands they would be less frightening. They are, of course, industrial operations on a significant scale, and employ thousands of people. Some are engaged in secretive, pioneering, dangerous work. But plenty of others are in much more mundane jobs. They arrive on the bus, or in white vans, playing their minor role in maintaining Britain's capability for waging nuclear war.

Writers are always trying to tune in to their own emotions, and the fear that buzzes somewhere in the hinterland between subconscious and imagination is a very powerful emotion. *Ah-ha!* thinks the writer, *here lies literary gold*. Something in me responds to this place so surely I should mine this seam? As soon as I started writing fiction, a year or so after leaving university, I began digging. But the ground didn't yield to my pen. I couldn't put together a decent story about the Atomic Weapons Establishment. I couldn't even conjure up a glimmer of an idea. The place was as impenetrable imaginatively as it was physically – the razor wire was doing its job. I let it go, moved on to other projects.

I lived for a while in Reading, and sometimes went on rides past the Atomic Weapons Establishment. I mentioned my obsession to a friend who'd recently graduated from the University of Reading. 'That place is weird,' she said. 'Do you know there's been a spate of suicides amongst staff in the last year or so?'

For a writer such a comment, made casually, not discussed at length, can spark a thought process that lasts for months, years. Sometimes the story is obvious. If you are fortunate, the story will be part of the spark itself. Other times, you will need to coax it out, like a nervous animal coming out of its hiding place. I felt sure that there must be a powerful novel about this group of suicides. Were they linked? If so, by what, or whom? The image of weapon-builders taking their own lives seemed to connect back to the regrets and guilt expressed by those who had designed the first atomic bombs. I'd been fascinated by AWE since that day when I rode past the Greenham Common Women's Peace Camp – here was my chance to write about it. And yet still the story couldn't be coaxed out.

Many years later, a meandering internet search took me to a site that outlined the many safety failings of the operations on the Aldermaston site, and the danger they presented to the local community. It reminded me of my friend's comment about the suicides, so I connected with her again and we exchanged a few emails, joking nervously about being surveilled by the Security Services. She spoke to some of her friends who had worked on the site and found out a little more about the suicides.

The truth, of course, was much sadder than any ham-fisted novel. There were no connections between the deaths, no dark conspiracy theories, no sinister plots. Just human frailty; depression, fear, sorrow. One scientist took his life shortly after retirement, the speculation being that he was unable to cope when he stopped work. Another hanged himself from a high building because he feared he had a brain tumour. A doctor told an inquest that his brain was healthy.

My fascination with the Atomic Weapons Establishment was morbid and immature. The cold, matter-of-fact industrial nature of the place seemed to resonate with the emotionless music of Joy Division that I loved as a teenager, and later with the paranoia of Radiohead. Aldermaston never yielded a novel for me because I never looked at it from any point of view other than my own. I suspect that those who work there fall into two camps: first, there are scientists, for whom the work is interesting and challenging; second, there is everyone else, who simply work to pay the mortgage and have found a way to cope with the hazards and the moral implications of the place.

For creative work to flourish there has to be an emotional connection. With Aldermaston I never made that connection, it existed in my imagination only as a set of dark and abstract ideas. A story comes from characters; characters from people. I cycled past the razor-wire fence and gazed in, that was all. Here was a landscape that intrigued me, but had nothing to impart.

Sky, Solitude

When we moved from Watlington to Henley, because of some paperwork machinations that meant we couldn't move straight into our new house, my family had to rent another house for six weeks. It was a small Victorian terrace on a busy road, unremarkable but adequate for such a short period. For me, the only interesting thing about this house was the sizeable mound of earth that sat squarely in what would best be called the yard – garden is too generous a word. The mound was perfect terrain for my rather disorganised army of plastic soldiers to play out their parody of the Second World War films I liked to watch on Sunday afternoons.

Never interested in military protocols, weaponry or international relations, my chief fascination lay in the way soldiers used the land to hide, pursue, attack. Barns were places to seek refuge, check ammunition supplies and have an argument about tactics; ditches were for crawling along, fields left your unit dangerously exposed, woods usually contained a sneakily hidden Nazi machine gun. Yes, every nine-year-old boy goes through the army obsession phase yet perhaps for me this was another, early, expression of an attraction to topography. A dry word, so let's try another way of putting it – from my smallest years I was attuned to the landscape, to outdoor physical space and its effects upon me. For a while, after abandoning the mound of mud, I created model landscapes using the Lilliputian kit of model railways, minus the actual railways. My soldiers preferred this cleaner environment for their battles, which they shared with my collection of Dinky cars. Though I liked creating a world in miniature (here is a novelist in development), I didn't have the patience to create anything very detailed – and I preferred spending my pocket money on sweets.

While the discovery of Aldermaston made a forceful impact on my imagination, when the Reading CTC groups headed north-west, beyond Pangbourne and Streatley, away from the Thames and the M4, I found myself in a landscape that immediately resonated with me. And over the years my love for it has only strengthened. I still ride and walk there when I can, and every time I feel replenished. I take the feel of this place away with me, keep it in my heart.

I'm talking about the Berkshire Downs, a range of chalk downland hills that forms part of a long wrinkle running across southern England. In the west are the

Marlborough Downs, in the east the Chiltern Hills that surround Henley. The Berkshire Downs' scarp slope faces north, its dip slope descends south towards ancient Savernake Forest and the hills of North Hampshire. While this ridge of rise and fall is defined by its geology, it is branded by a road. A white road that lies across the open green slopes, scratched into the chalky earth by ancient travellers. The Ridgeway, since 1972 a National Trail, is part of the Icknield Way, a loose road system that enabled traders to move goods across the country from the harbours of Dorset to the East Anglian coast. Alongside the Ridgeway are Neolithic, Bronze Age and Iron Age sites such as Avebury stone circle, Wayland's Smithy, Uffington Castle and the enigmatic Uffington White Horse, a beautifully sweeping shape cut into the chalk of a bald hill.

Through works like *Wildlife in a Southern County*, published in 1879, the nature writer Richard Jefferies, who grew up on a farm outside Swindon, is credited with bringing the Ridgeway to the attention of the British public, asserting its place in our history, and as a place to walk. Jefferies writes of the Ridgeway: 'A broad green track runs for many a long, long mile across the downs, now following the ridges, now winding past at the foot of a grassy slope, then stretching away through a cornfield and fallow. It is distinct from the wagon-tracks which cross it here and there, for these are local only, and, if traced up, land the wayfarer presently in a maze of fields, or end abruptly in the rickyard of a lone farmhouse. It is distinct from the hard roads of modern construction which also at wide intervals cross its course, dusty and glaringly white in the sunshine…'

Jefferies wrote novels and children's books, but it is his nature writing that he is remembered for. In his teenage years he spent much of his free time walking the Wiltshire countryside, particularly the Marlborough Downs and the western parts of the Ridgeway. At the age of 18, as he gazed out across the land from the top of Liddington Hill, Jefferies' sensitivity for nature coalesced into what he later described as a kind of transformative awakening. The natural world stirred in him a profound sense of magic and beauty. So deep was his love for animals, even when he became an apprentice gamekeeper in the hope of learning more about rural ways, he often found himself unable to shoot the wild creatures within his sights.

While failing in his duties as a gamekeeper, Jefferies read widely and developed an ambition to write. He produced a trio of novels, all published but none successful. Ironically, it was only when he moved to London, to the suburb of Surbiton, that his writing career took flight. He published a series of books that collected his articles on rural life in the villages around Coate in Wiltshire, where he grew up. These books, which included *The Gamekeeper at Home* and *The Amateur Poacher*, presented an intimate and honest reflection of the world he knew so well, written in a clean and simple style.

In later years he struggled with ill health, yet continued to produce books, many of which grew more daring in their style. *After London* was a fantasy about society returning to a medieval ruralism after the great city, and the Industrial Revolution it represents, has crumbled. His masterpiece, however, was *The Story of My Heart*, an autobiography written when his health was in terminal decline, in which he attempts to articulate what Paul Cudenec, in his 2015 preface, calls Jefferies' 'spiritual passion'. Jefferies begins his narrative with the day of his spiritual awakening on Liddington Hill, an event that at the time he was unable to translate into words:

> My heart was dusty, parched for want of the rain of deep feeling; my mind arid and dry, for there is a dust which settles on the heart as that which falls on a ledge... There was a hill to which I used to resort at such periods. The labour of walking three miles to it, all the while gradually ascending, seemed to clear my blood of the heaviness accumulated at home... Moving up the sweet short turf, at every step my heart seemed to obtain a wider horizon of feeling; with every inhalation of rich pure air, a deeper desire. The very light of the sun was whiter and more

> brilliant here… I was utterly alone with the sun and the earth. Lying down on the grass, I spoke in my soul to the earth, the sun, the air, and distant sea far beyond sight.

Jefferies' work, like that of John Cowper Powys, has not had the recognition and presence that it deserves. Both writers have become notable for the more famous writers they have inspired – William Morris in the case of Jefferies, Iris Murdoch in the case of Cowper Powys. Perhaps it's the element of mysticism that makes us uneasy.

Cowper Powys was another writer whose work sprang from the English landscape; his novel, *Wolf Solent*, presents an anarchic, primitive and sexual vision of the Dorset landscape he knew so well from personal experience. Cowper Powys was unabashedly opposed to modern forms of progress, including industry and capitalism, and revelled in medieval folklore. Jefferies was a little more accommodating towards progress, while warning of its dangers, but both writers were profoundly shaped by the landscapes of their youth, and both attempted to articulate a profound connection to the earth.

Place, for a writer, is a fundamental yet often under-considered influence. Under-considered because it is taken for granted. We all come from a place, all novels have a location, and that location defines much of the story, or at least its framework. And place always grounds a story, gives it a physical reality that readers can hang on to.

Many writers have a place that preoccupies them, that they go back to again and again. A fertile furrow. Often that place is called home. If writers like Jefferies and Cowper Powys, and scores of other writers and artists, build a lifetime's work from one place, it is because not only does that place expand to fill their imaginations, but there is also an emotional resonance for them. Everyone makes a mythology of their own lives, some turn it into stories. Early in his life, Jefferies had an ambition to travel across Europe, but shortly after landing in France he turned back, and never repeated the trip: far-ranging foreign travel wasn't necessary for his project. He would walk the paths and byways of his small patch of the world, examine them forensically, become part of the chalky earth's history. He wrote of feeling immortality on those Wiltshire hills, indeed of going beyond immortality. Time, with all its connections to mortality, the seasons, societal progress, was to be left behind for a mysterious higher state.

I find this an enticing idea but baffling. My own imagination struggles to elude the grip of time. Indeed, I revel in time, its loops and ellipses. Stories need time as much as they need place. On the Downs the landscape is moving at a different pace. Ancient history is not only on display, but also feels like it is hidden just beneath the surface of the land. It feels entirely credible for there to exist some shortcut to another era, a wormhole to antiquity. If M. R. James were not so preoccupied with East Anglia, he might have set some of his ghost stories effectively here, for if a character obsessed with Bronze Age peoples were to dig here and excavate some cursed relic, the windswept ridge would be a frightening place for a haunting.

The surface of the land may be different, the fields larger, the machinery more baffling, but when one stops to watch a combine harvester at work, it's not so hard to imagine a phalanx of men doing the same work in the same place, 500 years ago. From the ridge one can look out into the hazy distance, noting the aeroplane trails, the lines of pylons striding across the countryside, the villages that look like grey brushstrokes, and there is no sense of modern civilisation encroaching upon this place. Its height makes it impregnable. No one has ever wanted to live at the top of these hills, not since the days when castles were villages, anyway.

Cyclists can be either introverts or extroverts. Some prefer to ride in groups, others alone. I fall into the latter category. It's only when I'm alone and free of distraction that I can study the landscape and feel refreshed by it. So as soon as I secured my driving licence, and negotiated the loan of my mother's red Vauxhall Nova, I returned to the Downs with my bike stowed in the boot.

For walkers, the Downs are about old roads, trackways into the past. For the road cyclist the attraction is different. While the old roads run along the ridges, periodically sending paths off down the hillside towards villages, the new roads that Jefferies referred to criss-cross the land. Some stay low, connecting the settlements at the foot of the hills, others curl themselves around the hills, like the dragon that tempted Saint George. The most impertinent of these new roads launch themselves straight up a hill, over the top and down the other side, bisecting the ancient ridge road and cutting a break in the chalk.

Stop at the top of one of these hills and you will hear only birdsong, the distant drone of tractors, the wind riffling through copses of hawthorn and whitebeam. In summer, the expanses of barley and corn will shimmer and move; in winter, the same fields will be ploughed and studded white with chalk.

The openness is invigorating rather than intimidating; one doesn't feel exposed. One's eyes are always drawn upwards into the expansive skies, to swallows and starlings and the traffic heading to and from London's airports.

The Downs don't hide much from the cyclist. The landscape is easy to read, so it's easy to plan a ride, gauge an effort. The roads allow you to get into a rhythm. When there is one long ridge of hills, you choose how many times to go up over it. And you know whether you're on the steeper scarp or the more gradual dip slope, so you know what kind of climbing to expect. No nasty steepness will be sprung on you. Therefore it is a more meditative experience, simpler, serene. There is a pleasure in zipping back and forth across the ancient ridge road. By doing so the cyclist is saying that while he is in touch with the landscape of the distant past, he has the technology to bypass it: he is no longer enslaved to the land.

And there is a more mischievous aspect to being a cyclist too. For the road underneath my tyres, which may be old in its course but can only be a few years old in its surface, will cut straight through the ancient Ridgeway track. Walkers have to stop for the road's traffic, one can imagine their winces at having to encounter cars and garishly dressed cyclists. While the heritage industry would have you walk the Ridgeway and imagine yourself back in the Bronze Age, it's much more fun to subvert the prescribed ways to consume history. Don't follow any routes, cut straight across them, get lost.

Once, aged 18, I told a non-cycling friend that my plans for the weekend included a trip to a place called Letcombe Regis, a tiny village in Berkshire, from where

I was going to do a 50-mile bike ride. He looked at me, uncertain how to respond. He knew I was a cyclist, so the ride wasn't causing him confusion, it was more the idea of driving for an hour to get to somewhere to ride, when we were surrounded by perfectly good roads in Henley. I was racing at the time, doing daily training rides on my home roads, and though I may not have realised it at the time, I was getting bored – cycling should always feel like an adventure, an exploration. Racing was fun, thrilling even. But I missed the sense of discovery I got from those long meandering CTC rides a few years before.

West Ilsley, Berkshire. The quintessential Downland village; a jumble of red-brick cottages, bungalows, whitewashed walls and cul-de-sacs encircled by houses that once looked modern. The road that runs through the village is called Main Street, but the only saloon bar is in the snug interior of the Harrow Inn, whose drinkers look out on to a cricket pitch rather than cowboy gunfights. A little further along is the 14th-century church, humble in its architecture, built of flint and ashlar stone. Two horse chestnuts tower over the steepled gate.

I'm looking for a place to park. It's midday, midweek, and I have a day clear of work and childcare. The general administration of life has been swept into tomorrow; an afternoon of cycling lies ahead. On the roof-rack my bike is poised and ready. Beside me on the passenger seat is a rucksack full of high-carbohydrate, high-fat and high-sugar snacks. But my cycling kit is also in the rucksack; I need to get changed in the car.

Twenty minutes later, I click my helmet buckle, slide my sunglasses on and throw my leg over my saddle. Its engine ticking, like the heartbeat of an animal resting after a chase, the car is perched on a wide grass verge at the top of a set of rollers. I'm dimly aware, as I push off, that at the end of the ride I'll have to climb to this point, and that this will cause me more than a little pain.

At 43 I feel that I still possess some power, some speed. Given a bit more training and a bit less eating, couldn't I still hold my own in a race? Perhaps, or perhaps I'm kidding myself. One objective truth of getting older as a cyclist is that it takes longer to warm up. No one feels good at the very start of a ride but when you are young and fit you'll probably get into your rhythm within 10 minutes or so. The process is mysterious – at least to someone like me without any sense of scientific inquiry. While one's upper body settles into a familiar position, getting a feel for the bike and the road, one's legs turn stiffly. Pedalling is a conscious action, a little unnatural, and the aches from yesterday's ride have to slowly dissolve. Body melds to machine, machine to road. *Souplesse* – the cyclist's mantra that translates literally as flexibility but in this context is closer to fluidity – is regained. In the older cyclist this process takes longer, the initial aches more pronounced, and sometimes one thinks of simply turning round and going home. But eventually my body becomes that of a cyclist rather than a man on a bike. I'm in my element and everything is flowing in the right direction, albeit a little slower than I would like.

There is a psychological loosening too that happens at the start of every ride. In the first few miles one's mind is working on the same beat as before the ride, analysing, planning, plotting, worrying. Messages recently received are being processed and stored. Expected messages not received are being missed. One's internal monologue is a constant stream of exhortations to oneself – do this, call him, look into that. The usual modus operandi of the busy person, but it gently frays your nerves, leaves you frazzled. Sleep can be a relief from the chatter in your brain, at least in the sense that the subconscious mind transmutes it into dream images. But a much superior solution is sleep plus cycling.

On the bike, just as physical stiffness melts through pedalling, so one's thinking breaks down. With only the landscape and the weather around you, and at least a portion of your mind occupied with the act of making these two wheels travel forward safely, rational businesslike thought is curtailed, then switched off altogether.

Writing in 2016 in *The Paris Review* about the natural world and our age of anxiety, American writer and academic Megan Mayhew Bergman revisited the work of Alan Watts. A British philosopher and writer, Watts was born in Chislehurst, Kent, in 1915 and died in 1973 at Druid Heights, a bohemian community in Marin County, California, which tells you something of the journey his life took. Heavily influenced by Eastern philosophy, in particular Zen Buddhism, one of Watts' seminal works was *The Wisdom of Insecurity: A Message for an Age of Anxiety*, published in 1951.

Mayhew Bergman wrote, 'Watts feared, in 1951, that we had already left the body behind and entered into a more impotent existence centered in the mind. The human fascination with the past and future, and our "cerebral fantasies," was the sign of a maladaptive organ: the human brain. He believed that hyper-rationalizing our desires creates a vicious and taxing cycle, a habitual state of tension and abstraction that is actually a mental disorder. The "writhing and whirling" of the human mind, to Watts, is unnecessary and actually threatens man's happiness and survival by removing him from a physical existence, one more at home and peace in the natural world… The split between the brain and the body, Watts believed, is not unlike the split between man and nature. Both result in insecurity and anxiety.'

As a writer I often feel guilty about spending too much energy on planning, scheduling, ticking off actions, and too little time on daydreaming. The novelist Hanif Kureishi came to talk to a creative writing group I was part of a few years ago and the only thing I can remember from his talk was that he considered his job to be principally about lying on the sofa during the daytime, eating peanuts. He was having a tricky time convincing his children this was a worthy or viable full-time job. I find myself unable to head to the sofa during the middle of the day, there's always so much other stuff to be getting on with (90 per cent of which, of course, is procrastination to avoid the hard work of writing).

So I ride my bike, and the chatter disintegrates. When you are out in the hills, riding hard, feeling the sun on your face and the wind at your back, the hardest thing to do is compose a to-do list in your head. You may start, get two or three items clear, then notice a squirrel darting along a fence, or you might have to flick your wheel around some gravel on a bend. You duck a low-hanging branch, spring out of the saddle on a short rise. Take a drink. *Now, what was I thinking about?*

This is why I like riding alone. Not out of misanthropy, but because it is true solitude. Speech is not necessary, nor is conscious articulate thought. 'Other people' becomes one of two things – either memories, perhaps only an hour old, but memories all the same, or car drivers, encased in glass and steel. The car driver can never seem entirely real to a cyclist. They are not wholly visible, and the presence of their vehicle – however lovely the driver may be as an individual – is always an implicit threat.

So the lone cyclist moves through the landscape, a detached observer, with no social obligations. His mind can drift like the wind, it can focus on the next bend in the road or on the unfurling clouds. All the toxic ephemera of life can drain away to leave space for … what?

It's early March and a feather wind ushers thin streaks of white across an otherwise blue sky. Spring is already pushing through, green buds dot the hedgerows like confetti. Heading north towards Wantage, I spin through a wood. On one side of the straight flat road are beech, whitebeam, ash. On the other are rows of planted pine – cold, impersonal, dark. The sunshine now is only a pale yellow glow behind branches. At this time of year the cyclist knows to dress for cold weather, the sky cannot be trusted.

Out of the wood and the landscape opens before me, a wide vista of sand-coloured fields, bright green angles and the black scribbles of hedge and copse. The road drops and rolls, a gleaming mark on the hillside. There is nothing beside it other than a grass verge then field. No fence, no hedge, no buildings. A small absence but one that adds to the sense of openness. The aesthetic of the Downs is one of simplicity: field, sky, road, lone cyclist.

Picking up speed, I lean the bike into a succession of long, forgiving bends, enjoying the switch from side to side, and the way the bike comes alive when asked to perform. At low speed a good road bike can be a twitchy, awkward animal; only when it goes fast does it inspire confidence and supply thrills. Hands on the dropped part of the handlebars, head tucked into one shoulder, I churn a big gear to carry my speed off the descent and into the flat, then gently rising section ahead. Though the wind is light, on such an open stretch of road its effect is still noticeable. Here, it is neither foe nor ally, blowing across the road from the left. Sidewinds are only trouble when they are strong enough to need fighting, and when that happens it can be brutal, one's whole body becomes fugitive, rebuffing blows as it flees. That's not the case today and instead of fighting the wind I'm measuring it, trying to work out whether it will feel like riding through maple syrup or molasses when I turn into it. On a looping ride that winds up where it started, the impact of the wind should theoretically cancel itself out – riding against it will be matched by riding with it. Only it never quite feels that way.

I drop into Wantage and suddenly there are speed bumps, shops, drain covers, parked cars, a cacophony of signs, pedestrians staring at their phones and teetering on the edge of the kerb.

Here, for me, lies the useful contrast of the Downland landscape. One can climb to open space, feel connected to the simplicity of land and sky, then drop into the cosy hustle of towns and villages. Art comes from the messy complexities of human life, but the artist needs to carve out some space to reflect.

Of course, even on top of the purest chalk hill signs of human activity abound, and not just from ancient hands. Farming has defined this land, and its machinery is a visual reminder. In the watercolours of Eric Ravilious, who lived in Eastbourne, East Sussex, during the 1930s, the Downs are smoothly contoured and would be excessively pastoral but for the inclusion of simple yet sharp elements of human interference. Farm machinery, a barbed-wire fence, cement works, cottages – modernity is never far away. Ravilious was friends with the artist and designer Peggy Angus and based his painting trips at her cottage, Furlongs, at the foot of Beddingham Hill, and close to Virginia Woolf's cottage in Rodmell. From here Ravilious marched up onto the Downs, carrying a sketching easel and a brown canvas satchel, alert to the subtleties of topography and light that might give him his composition. Furlongs, and other modest buildings, feature frequently in his paintings but human figures are often absent. The emptiness of the buildings, looking out onto the emptiness of the hills, even in bright sunlight, is eerie. A house that sits alone in the open countryside naturally draws the eye. No matter how innocent or aesthetically pleasing, we can't help but wonder who lives there, what has happened there. These are the kind of blank questions that lead to stories. For the traveller the lonely house represents shelter, but we've all seen enough horror films to be a little wary.

Unlike his friend the surrealist painter and war artist Paul Nash, and that other lover of the Downs, poet, essayist and country writer Edward Thomas, Eric Ravilious was not a tortured soul. He had a cheerful, outgoing temperament, enjoyed his work, found time for dancing, tennis and love affairs, and was always whistling. The joy of being outdoors, trying to capture the simple beauty of his favourite countryside, comes through in his paintings. And yet there is just a hint of something darker at play in his imagination. When a barbed-wire fence runs out from the foreground of his picture, how does the concurrent feeling of conflict and division sit against the ancient chalk shapes beyond?

Another friend of Ravilious was H. J. Massingham, the writer who published many books on the history of the English countryside. The Downs were close to Massingham's heart too, and he revelled in the contrast between the solitude one could attain on the ridges and the (relative, for the 1930s) frenetic roads below. He summed it up in this memorable phrase – 'The road belongs to us, the Downs to the dead.'

Ravilious, though, did not shrink away from the road as a manifestation of modern progress. In *Wiltshire Landscape* (1937) a country road takes centre stage, spooling away into the distance, flanked by bare brown fields. A red van, most likely a Post Office vehicle, approaches a junction, a dash of colour in an otherwise muted palette. Though clearly a modern tarmac road, Ravilious gives it a white shine, so that it seems as old as the chalk tracks of his other works. The viewer's eye follows it over the shoulder of rising ground and, like the cyclist on roads he does not know, the viewer is intrigued as to what lies beyond. The open road is endlessly fascinating.

For Edward Thomas, the old roads were ingrained in his psyche. They were the arena for his emotional rise and fall. When he moved to a new house in Hampshire and did not settle there, Thomas felt depression bite. His response was walking, though tramping through the natural world did not always compensate for the poet's despair.

We now know that cycling, like most outdoor activities, is an effective salve for depression. There are innumerable stories of people who have lifted themselves out of a trough by taking up cycling, and their tales are backed up by robust science. Exercise has been proven to work as well as antidepressant medication, in part because it releases the chemicals that lift our mood – serotonin, dopamine and endorphins. And it's not only beneficial to those suffering from depression. A recent study in the *Journal of Clinical and Diagnostic Research* found that memory, reasoning and planning were all boosted after half an hour of cycling.

Other scientific studies show that time spent outdoors is also beneficial to mood, thereby confirming what cyclists have known for years, that getting out on your bike makes you happy.

The science, naturally, focuses on the physiological changes that happen when you ride and their consequential benefit for the rider's psychology. But I think there is also another aspect to cycling that fights depression, that of narrative. It's been shown that storytelling in psychotherapy is a productive way to allow patients to better understand their depression, and for the therapist to connect with their patient. A bike ride also has a story – that of exploration followed by a return to home. By its very nature a bike ride, like a story, is about movement. The cyclist covers more ground than the walker, and it's a freer movement, closer to flight. At times it may be a slog and the conscious mind begins to tick over, but at other times the cyclist is flying so fast he has to empty his mind of everything save the physical environment around him.

In his classic book *The Seven Basic Plots: Why We Tell Stories*, Christopher Booker analyses stories, their meanings and their archetypes. As the title implies, he suggests that there are only seven basic story structures. One of these he calls 'Voyage and Return'. Examples of this structure include *Brideshead Revisited*, *The Hobbit* and *Alice in Wonderland*. These stories all have a protagonist who travels to a strange new place, overcomes a threat or series of threats, and returns home changed by the experience. The ending is usually happy, but often tinged with sadness; with experience comes loss. It's a reassuring story shape for the reader because the final trajectory is always homeward, and home represents safety.

On every bike ride there is a moment when the rider turns for home. It may be clearly stated, such as staggering stiffly out of a café full of coffee and chocolate cake, or an almost imperceptible change of direction, but it always happens. It has to. To keep going in one direction means the destination is somewhere other than home, somewhere distant and possibly unknown.

My home, on this midweek jaunt over the Berkshire Downs, is my car, strewn with clothes and snacks, my glasses folded on the driver's seat. And my turn for home is in the town of Lambourn, famous for its connection to racehorses. I freewheel along its High Street, my reflection slipping between shop windows. A couple of teenage girls emerge from a convenience store, a pub is optimistically advertising jugs of ice-cold Pimm's, the sun bounces off the whitened road.

I head south-east on a B-road that follows the River Lambourn through Eastbury, East Garston and Great Shefford. Roads that follow rivers are always flat and their gentle curves mimic that of the river. With the wind nudging at my right hip, a diagonal tailwind, I'm riding fast, churning a big gear. The bike skips and rattles over the road's rashes and fissures. My eyes flick occasionally sideways, noting a pretty meadow or the sunlight dancing through a row of elms, but always return to the road. It's always about the road.

Solitude is not the same as loneliness. Nor is it the same as isolation. Solitude perhaps has more negative connotations than positive, because it gets associated with solitary confinement, solitude imposed on someone against their will, or reclusiveness, which is solitude made necessary by madness and fear. But solitude can be chosen, can be sought out. Indeed for an introvert, solitude is essential.

Have I had many ideas for stories while out on my bike? No, but I have thought of fragments, picked up images that remain in my mind until they find a home in a story, and I have seen places – like Aldermaston – that send my imaginative neurons firing. This is useful, for even if no story comes of it, the muscle of imagination is being exercised.

Sometimes I try to use the solitude of a bike ride to think through a problem, though this rarely works. Conscious, analytical thought is curtailed. Here's Tim Krabbe, from his novel about a fictional bike race, *The Rider*: 'On a bike your consciousness is small. The harder you work, the smaller it gets. Every thought that arises is immediately and utterly true, every unexpected event is something you'd known all along but had only forgotten for a moment.'

Emotions can still be very present for the cyclist but because the conscious mind has shrunk, emotions are not deconstructed and endlessly examined, they are transmuted into the physical world. Anger is pushed through the pedals into the tarmac, sadness reflected by the dark hills and the gathering clouds; joy is the sensory cacophony that makes you glad to be alive.

On the bike, do not consciously try to solve a problem, trust the breaking down process. Riding is like dreaming: the conscious mind shuts down, allowing something deeper to happen.

On a warm midsummer day, at a trendy cycling café in Spitalfields Market, East London, I meet up with landscape artist Matthew Webber. A resident of north-east London, Webber has been a racing cyclist as long as he's been a painter, with a healthy measure of success in both disciplines. We talk about the links between place and creative work and he describes how, for him, there is a direct connection between his favourite riding landscape and his work. The place he loves to ride is Epping Forest, the dense woodland wedged into the outer edges of London. From the busy roads that border it, the forest looks rather tame, rather managed, yet if one takes a bike onto its myriad of tiny paths, one is quickly submerged in a wonderful dark labyrinth.

Even if one spends time getting to know the layout, trying to memorise the paths, the forest is constantly changing, always throwing in little surprises. This may not be wilderness in its truest sense, but the careless traveller could easily end up going round in circles like those hapless actors in *The Blair Witch Project*. It is the opposite of my favoured landscape, the Downs. In the forest nothing is explained, nothing can be read at a single glance.

By connecting up local parks and paths, and the brutalist concrete underpasses beloved of sixties town planners, Webber can ride from his front door into the heart of the forest without touching a road. He rides for the same sort of reasons we all ride – for fitness, for fun, to escape. Riding off-road, he tells me, on sinewy paths littered with tree roots and fallen branches, demands total concentration. No dreaming, no philosophical analysis, there's no time for that. Concentration brings its own relief; it's a connection to the physical world. Body and mind working together to solve the problem of how to move fast through the environment. Everything else is purged, just for an hour or so.

On Webber's handlebars is a video camera, pointing upwards. It records as he rides, not the path as most off-road riders would, but the trees. When he gets home he downloads the recording and slows it down until he is looking at frame-by-frame images of the trees overhead. While his eyes were focusing on the path, the camera has focused on the canopy. Individual frames show random, abstract configurations of branches. When one catches his eye Webber will use it as the basis for a sketch that may then become a painting. With layers and layers of paint applied, then sanded back down, the original spidery branch shapes are usually impossible to discern in the finished work. But they are there, buried in the painting's history. Cyclists always desire movement, speed, and through this Webber has enabled 21st-century technology to capture a fleeting, ethereal picture of an ancient place, and all without any conscious intervention from the artist.

Fascinated by this process, I asked Webber if he ever went to other landscapes to paint. 'Occasionally,' he said, 'I can get away on my own for a few days to somewhere wilder.' Recently he loaded up his campervan with canvases, paint and bike and spent three days in Wales. Despite a lot of rain, he immersed himself for those three days in cycling and painting. My first reaction was that this sounded like bliss. Three days alone with only a bike and one's work. No children, no emails, no neighbours with whom to make polite conversation. Solitude, with all its space.

And yet solitude can grow oppressive. It didn't occur to me to ask at the time, but later I wondered whether he'd got lonely towards the end of the three-day stint. Surely solitude can turn sour, and we'll never know when that turning point comes until we try it. And when loneliness does begin to creep in, does that stifle the creation of art?

Sorted

I became a specialist in unrequited love. A school friend once told me that a mutual friend was in love with a girl in his class. 'They'd make a good couple,' I said. 'Why doesn't he ask her out?' 'Oh, no,' my friend replied, 'he doesn't want her to know, he prefers it that way.' At the time I was shocked, but later I understood, indeed saw something of this attitude in myself. Unrequited love is pure and idealistic. Whatever the initial spark, its early flames are heady and intense. Greedily sucking in oxygen, the fire cannot be doused by the disappointments to which normal, two-way human relationships are prone. Unrequited love will go on burning for days, weeks, years, slowly fading to embers then ash. It has its own internal energy; it sustains itself. Not to be confused with a cheap crush, a babyish infatuation nor simple lust (though lust is woven through it). This is love, deliciously gripping, one-sided, to be savoured, as my school friend realised before me.

While he was content to worship from afar, I caused myself piercing angst by fooling myself that there could be a chance of my affections being reciprocated. So I spent far too much time dreaming up wholly unrealistic schemes for persuading the girl of my originality and brilliance. When these schemes proved ineffective I tumbled into shallow troughs of depression and anger. From the outside these probably looked like typical teenage boy hormone surges but they were actually a celebration of my status as that most tragic of fools, the fool in love.

The object of my affections at this time was Elena. A fellow student on my Baccalaureate, she was Swiss, fluent in English, French and German, and possessed an elegance that set her apart from the English girls I was used to. Slightly taller than me, with short black hair, pale skin and very incisive blue eyes, she gave the impression of being older than us without being condescending, and richer than us without being ostentatious. She was friendly and kind but could also be inscrutable and a little chilly. On a few occasions she showed an underlying insecurity that naturally made her even more attractive.

I knew I had no chance of anything more than friendship – gently, she'd told me so. And yet still I went on, hoping that something might change her mind; having been submerged in the world of cycling, I was more naïve than most boys my age about the ways of the heart. The pain of rejection was only sharpened when Elena started seeing someone I knew, a six-foot champion javelin thrower called Jeremy. Even worse, Jeremy was impossible to dislike.

While this was happening I was racing my bike, and training hard. Because I saw Elena every day at college, I would come home with the memory of her fresh in my mind. As I sat in the kitchen, in my cycling kit, eating toast and drinking tea, I'd be working over everything I'd said to her during the day, analysing how I must have appeared. Oh, the agonising self-consciousness of a 17-year-old! By the time I wheeled my bike out of the garage I was ready to forget, the purgatory of a hard ride being much more satisfying than the purgatory of love.

For a racing cyclist the relationship one has with one's local roads is more like a marriage than the pointless idealism of unrequited love. Built over time, shaped by routine and habit, the cyclist's knowledge of the landscape where he lives becomes deep and intimate. He comes to forgive the landscape its flaws, acknowledging that beauty is a complicated thing. After all, who could love a place that has endless smooth roads, pretty villages, perennial sunshine and tailwinds? Such a place might be pleasant for a holiday but the cyclist's lasting love will always be for home. Just as Elena's occasional flash of anxiety made her more desirable, the rough edges of my training loops made them all the more interesting. Like a marriage, the relationship between a cyclist and his local landscape is two-way. The cyclist expresses devotion through regular visits, and pain. In return, the landscape gives the cyclist oblivion, a place to empty oneself, mentally as well as physically. On a more basic level, but still important, it offers athletic self-improvement. *If you know what you're doing*, the hills say, *I will make you stronger, fitter, faster*. This is the allure of the landscape, for the racing cyclist at least, this is its raw sex appeal: immediate physical gratification.

In cycling, pain has become a kind of totem. We glory in pain; we embrace and celebrate it. Pain sells product, it's a drug to which we're all addicted. Yet when cyclists talk about pain we're only really referring to a very specific sort of pain. When we ride up a steep hill, in order to maintain forward momentum we must push hard on the pedals. This requires our muscles to work so hard that we go into oxygen debt. Lactic acid is created, and lactic acid equals pain. Obvious, but worth stating because pain can mean many things. In the world outside cycle racing pain means grief, pain means chronic illness, severe injury. Such types of pain truly are the enemies of happiness. No glory here, no celebration, just the tough reality of being alive.

Cycling pain is a kind of pleasure, so we might say it's a masochistic pain. Rather like being in love, then.

Most days the bike led me downhill into Henley town centre, a short steep descent that was an exhilarating release of pent-up energy. With the nonchalance of all racing cyclists, but particularly 17-year-old racing cyclists, I would shift about in the saddle, adjust my clothing, shake out my heavy legs. Then, hurtling towards the implacable bulk of Henley Town Hall, which sits at the bottom of the hill, I sweep through a 90-degree bend, using as much of the road as possible without drifting into the path of an oncoming car.

To the north of town is a mile-long stretch of road known locally as the Fairmile, perfectly flat and straight, and because it's the main road to Oxford, there is a constant flow of traffic. On both sides there are wide grass verges, with parallel rows of trees and a bike path whose edges crumble into mud. Beyond, big houses hide behind privet hedges. Further along, there are fields rising up to the Chiltern foothills. Coming back, this is usually the scene for a glorious sprint finish, emptying the tanks. Going out, the effort is measured and tentative.

There is no need to settle into the bike, it being a natural extension of my body, but my legs are cold and stiff and therefore need to be coaxed back into cooperation. Rhythm is critical. There is a triangulation of gear size, cadence and wind direction, calculated instinctively, not analytically. The road helps, with its unusual construction in slabs, rather like a polished version of a military road, giving a bump every 20 metres that the bike absorbs. The trees too are at regular intervals. Front wheel bump, tree, front wheel bump, tree. Look up, look down, breathe, *breathe*. Cars swish past and my mind empties; all the day-to-day detritus, and the emotional fat encasing it, dissolving on the wind. Life can be reduced to the elements, one's body and one's machine. No mysticism, no Zen, no meditation, just a physical situation in which the cyclist is the central actor, yet doesn't need to make any conscious decisions. Pedalling, changing gear, steering and braking, all done unconsciously. The landscape folds itself around him and all conscious thought is obliterated.

At the end of the Fairmile the main road cleaves into a dual carriageway, the bike path ends and the cyclist is left under no illusion that he is being protected. So I turn off, taking a quieter road that leads me into the Stonor Valley. Through the hamlets of Lower Assendon and Middle Assendon and out into open farmland, and as the valley opens up so too do the possibilities for the ride. There are different ways to climb out of this valley, each with its own characteristics of gradient, length and landscape. And climb I must, for this valley is a groove in the land that has only one flat entrance – the way I've come in. A skein of sweat covers my forehead now, the stiffness in my legs has gone and I'm no longer aware of my pedalling. I have what we might call 'flow' – an enjoyable state but not one that will last.

On both sides gently contoured fields rise up towards tree-lined ridges. In autumn, these fields are rich; in winter, the chalk shines in the furrows as low sunlight skims ice-cracked puddles by the roadside. Occasionally I glance up, following the hedgerows up to the ridge. For a two-mile stretch the ridges on both sides are unknowable to a cyclist because there are no roads that cross them. There are footpaths, but I've never set foot on them. I imagine animals up there, watching my progress along this dangerous grey river. Halfway along the valley, a landmark of sorts is the wreck of a beech tree, blasted by lightning, blackened and twisted like a fighter plane shot down.

Just past Stonor House, a stately home only made interesting to me as a child by its secret hiding place for seditious Jesuit priests, I turn off the B-road onto a smaller lane, initially rutted and broken as it passes a farmyard. No white lines now, this road is too narrow, just curve after curve, and a gradient that works like a ratchet, slowly tightening. On my right, beyond an elegant iron fence, groups of deer stand nonchalantly in the grounds of the great house, chewing the grass or simply gazing into the distance, reflecting on the sheer futility of it all. They have no interest in me. Further up the hill there's a herd of Fresians, who take a similar position. We are not like the walkers who cross their field, we belong with the cars and the tractors, beyond the barbed wire. Often, when passing cows, I will let out as plaintive a moo as I can muster, but I rarely get much of a reaction.

This is one of those climbs that is possible to ride on the outer chainring, a higher gear, but only if your legs are feeling strong. I measure my progress by mundane milestones – fence posts, an entrance to a field. I'm familiar with all of them, and with every undulation of the road's surface. My legs are filling with lactic acid, my breathing becoming faster and deeper. Though still in the saddle, I'm starting to fight the machine underneath me, a strange and noble kind of wrestling, like two friends having a play-fight with an undercurrent of real violence. Rather than resting on the handlebars my hands are tugging at them, knuckles going white: push-me, pull-you. I head into a tunnel of high hedgerows, mercilessly strimmed into green walls, a scattering of gravel running up the centre of the lane, and the gradient slackens just a little. A driver would not notice this change, nor would a walker. Only a cyclist will feel this small change because he is so tuned in to that equation of road, gearing, power. The car driver would not notice but his car's engine would; the cyclist is the bike's engine, always assessing and recalibrating. It's just enough of a slackening to let me bring my leg speed up and steady my breathing. In front of me is the steepest ramp yet, the road curving eloquently away to the left and the hedgerows being replaced by open heathland, waist-deep bracken, ancient beech trees. An all-out effort, out of the saddle, mouth hanging open, eyes creased with pain. All style gone, all analysis erased. This is the purity of using my body to fight the slope. A brutally visceral tussle; every nerve ending aflame, every pedal stroke agonising, lungs scorched, the top getting closer, closer. Success means staying in the same gear and not falling off my bike when I hit the top.

For a racing cyclist the top of a hill is not a place of rest. It's where you measure your powers of recovery – a key indicator of fitness – or, in a race, it's a place to attack. If you have weathered your opponent's pace on the hill and are still riding within yourself, have a dig … click up through the gears and take off. Perhaps you'll never see them again. In training, though, this is the place to fall back into your rhythm and settle your posture, focus on your breathing growing shallow. Have a drink, raise your eyes, push on.

Cycling is a sport for romantics. Its legends are created through suffering and whenever you ride a bike you can understand that suffering. Everything important in cycling has a mythology. Just think of the always-shadowed Koppenberg, or the Arenberg cobblestones. Over the years we build our own personal cycling mythology, a kind of memory bank containing the images that are important to us – epic rides, races won or lost, roads that have punished us. I've been hopelessly in love with this sport for more than three decades and, yes, I have just such a gallery of images in my head. Rich, engaging, encouraging, it's my history on a bike. It comes with me on every ride.

If pushed, all of these images could be pinned to a time and a place. Except one. One image is a mystery to me and yet it's also extremely important. It pops up in my mind when I'm having breakfast before a long ride, when I'm filling my jersey pockets, or spinning away into an early-morning chill.

Here's the image: a lonely wooden shack, high in the Catskill Mountains; mist swirling through the treetops; a man sits on his porch eating a bowl of Grape-Nuts, that fantastically crunchy, malty breakfast cereal. The man is lean and tanned, dressed in plain black shorts and white jersey. A shining titanium bike stands next to him. His mind is clear, he can see what's ahead of him: it's a thousand-yard stare at a hundred miles of open road. For the next five hours he will be alone in the landscape. Just like yesterday. Just like tomorrow. I do not know his name, I think of him simply as the Grape-Nuts man.

Where did this picture come from? And why has it stayed with me?

As a child, when I wasn't riding my bike I was absorbing every book, magazine and video about cycling that I could lay my hands on. The most exotic pieces of literature were the American magazines. I remember *Bicycling* and *Winning*, but no doubt there were others. I pored over every page. Compared to the British magazines with their grainy black and white pictures of mud-caked Belgians sprinting into yet another unpronounceable Flemish town, these American counterparts were a blast of fresh air. The advertisements – as I remember them anyway – all seemed to feature a strip of sun-glistened tarmac, with a single central yellow line curving away through the redwoods. They held the promise of sunny days, smooth riding and empty roads. A true California nirvana. The feature stories too were suffused with a pioneering spirit. This was adventure, but with a European road racing sensibility: Jack Kerouac on a Pinarello.

The image of the Grape-Nuts man came from an advertisement in one of these magazines. I conjured a story to sit behind that opening image. It went something like this: every day this man trains in the mountains. Long, hard rides on his pristine titanium machine, always alone. In the afternoons he rests. He might go out to his workshop, where resides a fleet of perfectly maintained road bikes. Arranged neatly around the workshop are his spares. A shelf of Campagnolo derailleurs. A rack of lightweight Mavic wheels. A box of Christophe toe clips with oxblood-leather straps. Around the walls hang his tools, one for every conceivable job, and all gleaming, all in the correct place. Needless to say, his kit is spotless and his diet strict.

He is the epitome of a professional cyclist. And yet he is not a professional. He rarely leaves his mountain refuge. Three or four times a year, he loads up his car and drives to a local road race, where naturally he rides away from the competition. Before the victory ceremony he packs up and disappears. The organisers are used to it – he is such an enigma that he has become famous among local cyclists. His appearance at an event is an endorsement of its qualities. It's been said that some of the tougher road races have been created just to tempt him out of the woods, like a trail of food laid for a brown bear.

Across America, there are elite racers and team managers who remember the period when he dominated the country's biggest events. Some of them knew him personally. No one knows the reason for his self-imposed exile. The cycling media have given up trying to find him. His peers don't often talk about him, but when they do it's with a hushed awe and more than a little fear. What if he makes his comeback? What scrappy prizes will be left for everyone else if he re-emerges? For now, they are safe. The Grape-Nuts man is still training, still a recluse. And yet every time they arrive at a bike race and see a car carrying a single titanium bike, a pang of anxiety twists at their guts.

I suspect that for many racing cyclists, the training is more enjoyable than the racing itself. The lone rider punishing himself in all weathers, absorbing the landscape, inflicting pain on himself. There is a certain ascetic glamour to it. Of course, all athletes punish themselves and put in the time, but cyclists can regularly disappear alone into the hills for four or five hours. Training is an addiction, a need. When it's going well, you feel every sinew in your body and mind getting tougher, leaner. You feel powerful enough to destroy your rivals. When it's not going well, when you're glued to the road, you tell yourself that you're weak, that the only solution is more training. More miles, more hills, more pain.

The road winds slowly upwards from Turville Heath, a hedged groove once more, with expansive views over the Stonor Valley flashing past at every break in the hedge. I've only gained a hundred metres of height but I feel closer to the clouds scudding overhead, more exposed to the wind and rain and sun. When a road runs along a ridge one has the sense, utterly irrational, of precariousness. Through the village of Northend, where, at the age of 13, I got drunk on cider and kissed a girl I'd previously thought far too beautiful to cast so much as a glance my way. Past a swampy pond and some solid homes with BMWs on gravel drives, ivy-clad outbuildings and picket fences.

At Christmas Common there is a drunken crossroads. Head across it and the road will climb over bare hillside towards the summit of Watlington Hill, with its secret bunker and a puddle-strewn car park for those wishing to walk to the White Mark. I could stop there, my cleated foot clicking onto the tarmac; I could gaze out across the Vale of Oxford, at the same view I drank in as a child – the western skies, horizons with the promise of freedom and love. But I don't go there. I am a racing cyclist now, I do not stop.

And as a racing cyclist, landscape is reduced to a set of contours, brushed by the weather, but otherwise existing only as an abstraction. I am dimly aware that there is a complex world on either side of this tarmac ribbon, a multitude of lives in every street, but all that matters is the road and how much it hurts, how much harder my body is becoming. There could be purple sheep in the fields and cottages made of gingerbread, but the single-minded will see nothing other than the road ahead. Perhaps that's the reason my racing career ended prematurely and I became a writer instead. I'm too easily distracted by the world of endless joys, sadnesses, ideas. I want to stop and lead the purple sheep into the gingerbread house, see what they do.

Ridge roads often feel fast; perhaps it's the promise of the descent that awaits your momentum. Here, on Watlington Hill, there are six different ways to descend to the flatlands surrounding the village, each subtly different in gradient, width, road surface. And each hill has its own identity; they are named Britwell, Sliding, Howe, Watlington, Aston and Kingston. Of these, Sliding Hill is my favourite. The name reflects the impression that the bulk of the land has slid downwards, creating a descent that starts gently then plunges steeply at its end, amid dark bramble. To stay on the bike I would have to squeeze the brakes, keep my tyres off the patches of treacherous gravel, squint into the sudden gloom and hope not to meet any tractors coming the other way. But this evening I'm going to stay high for as long as I can, following the ridge.

The nuclear bunker isn't the only secret of this landscape. At Aston Rowant there is Cowleaze Wood, which in late spring is ablaze with bluebells, yet on a heavy day can be ominously dark and still. Broken only by the stripes of firebreaks, scattered within the wood are the remains of a sculpture trail, abandoned for lack of funding. Some of the art has been dismantled and removed, leaving ghostly empty spaces; some has been left to slowly rot. Surrounded by breezy downland and ancient deciduous woodland, this mainly conifer forest is rather forbidding. Walk into its centre and you will feel a chill that is more than physical. If you're brave, and you don't get disoriented, you may eventually come to a corner of the wood where the light bursts in and a huddle of beech trees marks its boundary. There is a gate here; beyond it a footpath slices across open farmland, dropping into a small valley. A sign beside the gate politely requests that you stay on the footpath and keep your dog on a lead while walking through the Wormsley Estate.

This is a very British secret place. There is no through road along the valley, no tall fences or security guards, no signs telling you to keep out. Quite the opposite – a footpath runs right through the estate. Privacy, for the estate's wealthy owner, is assured through ordinariness. Just another quiet dip in the land, more fields, more woods, a big old house with its own cricket pitch.

Growing up, I used to imagine the owner, Sir John Paul Getty Jr, as a shambolic old man shuffling around his mansion in slippers and dressing gown while the farming families who lived in the tiny estate cottages doffed their caps and pretended to be quintessential English folk. For Getty the estate must have been a refuge, so turbulent was his life. He bought it in 1986 from the Fane family, a grand old aristocratic family who have seen more than their fair share of cap-doffing, and set about renovating the estate, including the creation of a replica of the Oval cricket ground – Getty, who had British-American dual nationality, fell for cricket after being introduced to it by Mick Jagger.

By 1986 Getty had survived divorce from his first wife, the death by heroin overdose of his second wife, the kidnapping of his eldest son, and a long period of drug addiction. Shortly before buying Wormsley he checked himself into a London rehab clinic, where Margaret Thatcher visited him and told him not to let things get him down.

Getty's son, John Paul Getty III, was 16 when he was kidnapped in Rome in 1973. He was imprisoned for five months in an Italian mountain hideout while the kidnappers tried in vain to persuade his grandfather to pay the $17 million ransom. Eventually they lopped off one of his ears and sent it to his grandfather, one of the wealthiest men in the world, who then reluctantly paid a negotiated ransom. After that experience, perhaps not surprisingly, John Paul Getty III slipped into alcohol and drug addiction. In 1981 he suffered liver failure and a stroke as a consequence of taking valium, methadone and alcohol and was left a quadriplegic.

Father and son both died at home on the Wormsley Estate, in 2003 and 2011 respectively. John Paul Getty III's younger brother, Mark, still lives at Wormsley today.

Click, click. Up a couple of gears as the road dips away from fairytale forests and tragic billionaire mansions. I lower my chin a fraction, tuck my elbows in, fly down this slight descent, legs spinning carelessly, eyes streaming. On both sides there are high landscaped banks of earth dotted with young trees. Where there are roads there is human design. The descent throws me out onto a bridge across the M40. Staying low to minimise the effect of the wind I know will now hit me, I swivel my head left, like a swimmer taking a breath during front crawl. Below me is the wide incision of the Stokenchurch Gap, where the motorway blasts through the hillside, creating a deep canyon with chalk walls.

A little further along the ridge is a tower, a tall shaft of dreary beige cladding topped with satellite dishes and a tangle of aerials. Intercepts messages from the Soviets, my father used to say, and I liked this idea. Streams of coded Communist babble being plucked from the sky by this silent bastion of Britain's defence. I imagined other such towers, standing proudly on hills across the country like listening trees. That such a secret and important installation had been planted in the corner of an ordinary field a few miles from my house was exhilarating. It gave me a sense that this landscape was special, that even the wind carried dangerous secrets.

If the natural shape for a bike ride is a loop, however ragged and deformed, as soon as the rider begins turning through the landscape he defines the shape of that loop. By turning north onto the ridge road I'm already defining the rest of the ride; to get back to Henley I will drop into the Hambleden Valley, which runs roughly parallel to the Stonor Valley, then power along the Marlow Road, beside the Thames. A route of 20 miles or so.

Not far past the Cold War sentinel, I encounter the M40 again, sweep right through a junction and sprint out of the saddle across the motorway bridge. After taking me through the cool air of Hartmoor Wood, the lane skirts a village cricket pitch (not a replica of the Oval, as far as I know), and a shuttered pub. With the road dropping away again it's impossible not to go fast here. My legs are flying round, elbows at right angles as I grip the bottom of the bars and my wheels skip over pockmarked tarmac. At this speed one becomes less cognisant of the weather, or the broader sweep of the land. All that matters is driving this machine forward. There is pain in my legs but it's blurry, only enough to elicit the edge of a grimace, and my speed is its compensation. I catch myself thinking, if only Elena could see me now, then immediately obliterate this ridiculous thought – what, if she could see me now she'd leave her javelin-throwing hunk and come to bike races with me every Sunday, massage my legs, throw her arms around me after the finish? For fuck's sake!

The road curls along the edge of Mill Hanging Wood and a view is revealed of a precipitous hillside, a valley, a rust-coloured village. Then, ahead, perched on top of the hillside is the first symbol of the surreal feeling of the Hambleden Valley. A windmill made of white clapperboard, hexagonal, with square dark windows on each side. Its sails haven't moved for years. It is a home, a motif of past industries and of happy endings, for this is where *Chitty Chitty Bang Bang* was filmed.

The village at the foot of the hill is Turville, picturesque and famous for being the fictional village Dibley, home to Dawn French's charmingly mischievous vicar. When I was at school, one of my friends, a tall, striking girl with cropped hair, was the daughter of Turville's real vicar, a good-natured and radical man who was the inspiration for the television series. The vicarage plays a part in my own mythology, for I lost my virginity at a party there, though sadly not to the vicar's daughter with the cropped hair.

So many films and television shows have been filmed in the villages of this valley that the place has an unreal feeling, as if it has been designed and built, a stage-set version of 'rural England'. A favourite family game when I was growing up was being the first to spot a Hambleden location on TV. Easy to get to from London, with many tiny lanes climbing away from the valley road, and a succession of pretty hamlets, it's easy to see why location scouts have this place circled on their maps. A vigorous stream, Hamble Brook, runs down the valley through lush water meadows, sometimes ducking into ancient stone culverts. In periods of prolonged rainfall the stream luxuriates in the space of the meadows, covering grass and wildflowers. The valley road stays on slightly higher ground, following the stream towards the Thames. On both sides of the valley, as the ground rises and becomes safe from flood, there is a band of fields, beyond them dense woods.

The buildings are mostly farmers' cottages constructed of local brick and flint, small square windows, smoke curling from chimneys, wooden rocking chairs on flagstones…

See how easy it is to find yourself in a period drama? Never mind that there are probably more lawyers and financial consultants living here than farmhands and carpenters, these cottages evoke a sense of permanence and cosiness that one knows is a kind of deception, but seductive nevertheless.

The village of Hambleden itself is a perfect embodiment of this duality. Settled in the base of the valley with a diminutive stone bridge straddling the stream, it is arranged around a gently curving road, with a church and a pub on either side and a broad chestnut tree that casts its shadow over the churchyard. There is a post office-cum-shop, a water pump, a patch of allotments and, behind the pub, yet another cricket pitch. Every cottage is well-preserved, apparently aware of its place in this museum of English country life. There are some houses that are less than a hundred years old, but they are kept out of sight, away from the cameras.

Entering Hambleden does not feel like stepping back in time so much as stepping into a small theme park, where the kids will get bored very quickly. Like a theme park there is a robust commercial operation going on here. The entire village and much of the surrounding land is owned by a Swiss billionaire, Urs Schwarzenbach, who bought the estate for £38m from Henry Smith, heir to the WHSmith fortune. The cottages are leased to sitting tenants and the whole village is frequently hired out to film and television companies. One may come here and find the road covered in imported mud, or the hillsides sprayed with artificial snow. Eccentric detectives, murderers, American GIs resting between engagements with Nazis, one can see many worlds in Hambleden's versatile streets. The locals are paid £50 every time their TV aerials are removed for filming.

The idea of a village has long been central to English identity. Ruralist H. J. Massingham wrote, 'Where does man belong? He belongs to his own place which he has almost lost. In his own place he is able to be himself; in his own place he is in touch with what is beyond space and time. The simple Christmas story affirms this to be so. Its tale of the infinite lodged in a village is absolute truth in a nutshell.' In the first half of the 20th century, as Britain's rapid economic and industrial growth began to irredeemably alter our conception of the nation's landscape, Massingham and others pointed to the village as the bedrock of our society, being composed of a physical triangle – church, houses, fields – that corresponds to God, Man and Earth. Some have inserted the word 'public' before houses, the pub being more of the countryman's spiritual home than his own house. Implicit in this analysis of the ideal rural community is the authority of the squire who, *naturally*, is benevolent towards his peasants while embracing new technologies to make his land efficient. Factories, suburban sprawl and a politically restive working class all threatened this ancient balance.

Almost a century after Massingham was writing, Hambleden is a rare and strange continuation of the English village. The possession of a man who made his fortune on the money markets, its principal function seems to be to preserve an aesthetic, a collective nostalgia too tidy, too organised to bear much relation to historical reality. Compared to the scruffy working reality of Watlington, Hambleden always seemed to me utterly unreal. Never more so than when riding through it on a bike. With sunglasses and helmet on, aboard my glittering machine, I feel like a spaceman, dispassionately observing a society through its museum exhibits.

Did I, at the age of 17, see myself living in a place like this, in a cottage with roses around the door, drinking in the saloon bar of the village pub with Elena beside me? No, but at 17 I had very little conception of anything other than bike racing and girls. In the former I had the commitment, but not the intelligence, lofty ambitions with no basis in the reality of my abilities; the same applied in love.

Hold that wheel, hold that wheel! The heels of his shoes, cranking out the rhythm, his spokes visible as the wheel turned, every detail taunting me as the tarmac opened up between us. Inch by inch, the gap grew. My legs were screaming, my lungs wanted to squeeze out from my ribcage, my face was wracked with pain. I was giving everything, and this rider was still getting away from me. The hill was steep – 12 per cent – but short. A junior road race, some time in the summer of 1992. The course was a 10-mile lap, to be covered five times. On each lap we had to climb this hill, known locally as the Blowing Stone Hill. A narrow lane rising up onto the Berkshire Downs, covered by a canopy of trees, it's an unusual climb because it goes in a straight line up the hillside, making you think that it's relatively easy. Difficult climbs usually have to contort themselves back and forth. But by the time you're halfway up Blowing Stone your legs are saying you've been deceived. The finish line of the race was at the top of the hill. It was only the second lap, and I was going backwards.

Climbing was not my strength as a racing cyclist. Anyone who rides a bike knows how hard climbing is. On a hill (never mind a mountain), our limits are clear to ourselves, and to everyone around us. For those new to cycling, hills are a source of anxiety. And it doesn't get much better with experience. If you're bluffing about your fitness, whether in a race or a ride with your friends, the hills will find you out. So to see climbing done effortlessly is inspiring, far more than seeing a *rouleur* rolling along on the front of the peloton on the flat, or the hurtling antics of the sprinters.

The Blowing Stone race was a perfect example of my wrong-headed approach to racing. Two weeks later, I was due to compete with an English Schools team in a stage race in Holland. I knew the stage race would be flat and fast, yet there I was in a hilly race getting spat out of the peloton. I had the ambition to be successful in bike racing but I wasn't clever enough about it. My training lacked focus, my diet was terrible. Needless to say I was underprepared for the Dutch race and did embarrassingly badly. On one stage we hit a cobbled section after 10 kilometres and while my teammates powered along at the front, I bounced unceremoniously off into a ditch.

It's hard to articulate in prose the feeling of racing a bike. Many books can give you information about this – he attacked there, he dropped back here – but few have managed to convey the feeling of being in the peloton. I can think of only two – *The Rider* by Tim Krabbe, and Matt Seaton's seminal memoir *The Escape Artist*. Perhaps bike racing is such an elusive experience to pin down in words because it is more about knowledge than visceral, physical activity. *The Rider* and *The Escape Artist* both allude to this, to the sense of bike racing being a closed community, with its own culture and set of behaviours. If you're inside that community, you already understand what it means to race. And if you're on the outside, no amount of reading (so the logic of the racer goes) is going to explain to you what it feels like to race. You can ride all the sportives and mountain challenges you like, they're not races.

My racing career, which ended when I was 19, was modest. At the time I blamed a lack of natural talent. In recent years, having got to know a few elite racing cyclists, I've come to understand just how strong their competitive urge is. Without it an athlete will never drive himself to the top of his chosen sport. Impossible. I didn't have that competitive spirit. As a rather self-conscious, introverted teenager I was more interested in saving face. My objective for a race was usually to avoid being dropped by the peloton. I tended to give up too easily, to look for a way out of a tough situation.

My last race was ended prematurely by a deer. It was July 1992 and I was in fairly good physical shape. I'd driven, alone, down to Hampshire for a 60-mile race on a circuit that was rolling without being brutal. I knew that if I could hang in there over the hills, I'd have a chance in the sprint finish. Winning was probably out of my reach, but a Top Ten was entirely possible.

Halfway through the race we were zipping along a country lane. I was still recovering from a climb in which I'd slipped backwards, so was near the back of the peloton. Then suddenly there was a shriek of brakes, shouts, swerving bodies. A crash. No, there was no crunch of bodies, no wheels flying in the air. Everyone had managed to stay on their bikes but the incident brought us all to a standstill. In unison we changed down a couple of gears and got out of the saddle to labour our bikes back up to speed.

I found myself in a group of about 10 riders. The peloton had disappeared up the road and we faced a chase back. Knowing, without the need to discuss it, that we had to work together, we began doing through and off, each taking a turn to break the wind and set the pace then swinging off and joining the back of the group to take a rest. The rhythm we were setting was good; if the peloton eased back – as often happens in races at that level because the pace is erratic – we would surely be able to reattach ourselves to the back of the chain?

My legs felt good, I was able to drive the pace of our small group of unfortunates. Then we hit a hill in open countryside, where we could see that the peloton were still a long way off. All my fight evaporated. The chase was futile. I sat up and let the group ride away from me, then turned around in the road and headed for the showers.

Once the race had finished I found out that the incident had been caused by a panicked deer jumping into the road and scaring the life out of a couple of riders. I also learned that the group I had been riding with did make it back to the peloton half a lap later.

Why had I given up so easily? Because my hunger had gone. Bored by racing and by training, I was stale. I no longer even cared about the humiliation of 'packing', the term we used for dropping out of a race. On the drive home I decided to take a few weeks' break, rest up, then come back, hopefully refreshed. I took the break, but I never went back to racing.

During that summer of 1992, for the first time cycling felt like it was narrowing my life instead of broadening it. For two years I'd been combining studying for a Baccalaureate with racing and training. While I could maintain the delusion to myself that my monkish lifestyle would pay dividends when the big races came around, I was happy to eschew a social life. When the big races didn't go as expected and I was forced to recalibrate my perception of how good I was, the equation didn't seem so fair: if I was putting in all this effort just to come sixth in a local race, was it worth it? I'd wanted to get on the British team going to the World Championships in Mexico, but the reality was that I was nowhere near that level. Failure colours our lives slowly, its deepening is almost imperceptible. I didn't make excuses so much as gradually turn my energies elsewhere; I worked hard for my exams, I got a girlfriend who had no interest in cycling, I reconnected with school friends I hadn't seen for a while.

If, that summer, cycling felt increasingly at odds with the rest of life, the conflict was brought into sharp focus at the end of May of that year. My friends and I had long been devotees of the guitar-based indie band. From Joy Division through The Smiths to The Pixies and The Fall, we'd flirted with more rebellious splinters of punk and post-punk, and I'd even had a brief Goth phase, but it was all pretty standard stuff for small-town teenage boys. In 1992, though, things were starting to change. Dance music culture was beginning to bleed into the sound of some of the most important guitar bands. Primal Scream's seminal album *Screamadelica* was released towards the end of 1991 and had several tracks that combined spaced-out optimism with acid house beats. The Stone Roses' 'I Am the Resurrection', an eight-minute single released in March 1992, was a shape-shifter – the first four minutes were bombastic rock and then the track broke down into a rollercoaster instrumental that blended funk with blues and made you want to get up and dance. Acid House had started in the late eighties as a genuinely underground scene, inspired partly by New York's dance music culture, but also as a reaction to the sugary excesses of the New Romantics and the bland commercial crap shown every Thursday on the BBC's *Top of the Pops*. Acid House had no personalities, just a codified language and a collective sense of breaking free. It was also, of course, wrapped in the drug after which it was named, and Ecstasy too.

By the first years of the nineties, Acid House had morphed into 'rave' and those canny enough to spot a trend had seen the commercial opportunities in the scene. Promoters put on events in nightclubs, and for a while everyone seemed to benefit – punters, DJs, security firms, drug dealers…

In the summer of 1992 the illegal rave scene was still growing. While promoters, bands and record companies were tuned in to the nuances of the rave scene, the authorities had barely registered its existence. This all changed over the second May Bank Holiday weekend.

Word got around that a big free party was being organised, and if you were to ring a certain phone number you'd get through to an answer-machine message that told you the location. A convoy of New Age Travellers had been moving about the West Country throughout that spring, putting on small free festivals. At the end of May, pushed out of Somerset by the local authorities, they drove into Worcestershire and set up camp on Castlemorton Common, near Malvern. This was to become the scene of the biggest free – and illegal – festival in Britain. An estimated 30,000 people travelled to the site, prompting comparisons to Woodstock. Over the long weekend the party sprawled over farmland and common land. Locals felt, understandably, as if they were the victims of an alien invasion. The festival had several sound systems that played continuously through night and day. The crowd grew, absorbing cars full of kids who'd never been to a free festival before, Londoners and suburban kids for whom this was what Glastonbury should have been like, wild and free and rebellious. The party became a gathering of the tribes. All the underground dance music scenes gathered at Castlemorton, united by the infamous 'repetitive beat' that soon after became the basis for the Criminal Justice Act.

Taken by surprise, and fearing violence if they tried to intervene physically, the police took the decision to watch from a distance. The event was so huge that there was little they could do to shut it down. Castlemorton was a turning point in the rave scene. National newspapers were hysterical in their condemnation and the British government reacted with the legislative knee-jerk of the Criminal Justice Act. Parties had to be licensed, ticketed, insured. They moved into nightclubs, industrial units and unsuspecting leisure centres, and for those who'd been going to illegal raves for several years, the fun was over.

Artist Jeremy Deller created a flow diagram called *The History of the World, 1997–2004*, in which he charts the connections between northern brass bands and the rave scene of the nineties, the former being the musical expression of industrial 20th-century Britain and the latter the expression of post-industrial 20th-century Britain. Castlemorton is there, in capital letters, near the centre of the diagram. Around it are the words: 'Festivals, The

Miners' Strike, Civil Unrest, Summers of Love, Advanced Capitalism.'

My friends went to Castlemorton. On the day after the Bank Holiday Monday they came into college, glassy-eyed, and were able to say, *we were there*.

Where was I that weekend? At another fucking bike race.

Later that summer, I got my dose of wildness. The rave my friends and I were headed to in Otterbourne was visible from the M3, a halo of strobing lights on top of a bare hill. Coming off the motorway, we found that the road we thought we could take to get there was blocked by police, so we turned away and found a nearby cul-de-sac. Other ravers had parked there too and were loitering around their cars, doors open, beats and bass escaping into the night air. The suburban houses kept their doors shut and their curtains drawn. One could sense the shuddering inside.

Leaving my trusty Vauxhall Nova behind, parked haphazardly in front of someone's drive, we started walking. The police had closed the road to the rave but were letting those on foot get through – they didn't yet have any power to stop us. There was a curious gleeful silence as we bowled past the line of policemen.

We walked along a country lane in a low valley. All around were groups of ravers, chattering away at amphetamine pace. MA-2 jackets, hooded sweatshirts, tie-dye T-shirts, baggy jeans, beat-up old trainers... We were suburban kids bored of being told what to listen to by radio stations and record companies. Illegal raves were our way of breaking free, of rebelling, and it was private property that was threatened. Which was why, in the end, the rebellion was put down by the government. It wasn't the wholesale consumption of drugs they were scared of, but the midnight invasions of private land.

Through the high summer gloaming we walked, beckoned by the thud of bass from the hilltop and an occasional flash of light. Into a field and through a small city of caravans, ancient painted buses, tents and battered cars. Groups of people sat smoking around campfires, dealers stood to one side of the stream of kids climbing the hill, calling out their merchandise. There were no police here; they were happy to stay back at the roadblock. For them it was a better gig than dealing with football hooligans.

The music grew louder, chaotic, hypnotic. Basslines so powerful they shook the pair of oak trees we ducked underneath. Beats that eddied and ricocheted. There was no human voice, and that was part of the appeal. Acid house and all its subsequent incarnations was a sonic, not an emotional, experience. The music was made by machine and sounded like it. Truly it felt right for that time. The end of the century was approaching – we didn't want swaggering guitar bands who knocked out versions of Beatles' songs, we wanted something that felt like the future. Hardcore made you happy because it made you want to dance. Ecstasy intensified this relationship by releasing a flood of serotonin into your brain. As the MDMA filtered into your bloodstream the music seemed to lift your feet from the ground, the music became three-dimensional, a rich and physical force. For a few hours we were all synaesthetic. There were no interruptions and there was no theatricality, no building to a climax or going off for encores. The DJs played in rotation from nightfall to sunrise, mixing one tune into the next, seamlessly maintaining a flux wave of sound.

Emerging from the darkness of the oak trees we found ourselves on the bald hilltop we'd spotted from the motorway. Two sound systems, each on the back of a flatbed lorry, had been set up about 300 feet apart. One was playing hard techno, the other acid house. From the top of the cab of one of the lorries a single spotlight projected a powerful beam of light into the sky, at intervals swivelling around. We smiled at each other, picked a spot, and began to move our feet.

Within an hour it began to rain, just lightly, just enough to create an entrancing effect in the beam of the spotlight, and we kept on dancing, grinning like idiots, chewing gum and shaking hands with strangers. It felt like it was a long way from a bike race, and I enjoyed that. I was rebelling against myself. Only now, comparing the two, do I see that it wasn't so dissimilar; I was on a downland hill, escaping, living within my senses, pushed on by rhythm. And if a bike was a piece of technology that might unlock the secrets of the English landscape, why couldn't a New Age Traveller's sound system perform the same function?

If our lives are stories, our experience is a narrative, we are following an arc. And like a story the curvature of that arc is composed of thousands, millions of tiny moments, all nudging us forward. Look back on your life and you can define pivotal times, when the trajectory of your life changed for good. For me, that summer of 1992 was pivotal. Freed of the pressure of racing my bike I found new friendships, love, rebellion. I found too that there are more ways to lose yourself in the land than on two wheels.

In 'Sorted for E's and Whizz', Pulp's Jarvis Cocker wrote about losing an important part of his brain somewhere in a field in Hampshire, and took a dig at the rave scene for being hypocritical – idealistic and friendly when everyone was coming up on their pills, less so when everyone's coming down and you're trying to get a lift home – and essentially meaningless. Yet this is missing the point. No 18-year-old kid went to a rave in a field looking for meaning, at least not consciously. And there was a sense of gender neutralisation too; the purpose of a rave party was to dance, not to pursue the opposite sex. For all the media hysteria about the dangers of Ecstasy, the scene felt like a safe haven from the prevailing politics of conflict and triumph. The scene was about escape and anarchy, defying older generations. The Cold War was over, capitalism was victorious. The brassy, troubled eighties of the Iron Lady had become the shambolic nineties of the Grey Man, John Major. We were hungry for the future and for a sense of a collective spirit. Those who shared those times are happy to have left a part of their brain somewhere in a field in Hampshire. As long as the crackly wires of memory go on transmitting, I can take myself back and remember what it felt like to be there and to feel such naïve optimism. It was beautiful.

Though I took my bike to university, I barely rode it. I'd intended to join the local cycling club, get fit again, do some racing. Perhaps if the academic year started in spring, I might have done so. But by the time I'd worked out the basics of living away from home, it was October and the racing season was over.

Who am I kidding? I was never going to race again, at least not up there in Norwich. The change in me that started that summer of 1992 continued throughout the autumn. A new place and new friends meant the opportunity to reinvent myself. To some degree we were all reinventing ourselves, just not admitting it to each other, so everyone held their secret transformation tight to themselves.

After the social maelstrom of the first term, it was music that brought my group of friends together. Because jungle, house and acid were still relatively underground, and very much seen as associated with drugs, there wasn't anything for us at the Student Union. We might go for a couple of drinks before heading to a nightclub in the city. We got to know local DJs, promoters and drug dealers. We drove through the empty Norfolk nights to illegal raves in Thetford Forest, or on disused industrial estates in Great Yarmouth.

But though we probably got to know far more local people than most of our peers, some of whom existed entirely within the campus, there was still a strong sense of us and them. On our part the condescension of the naïve and arrogant, young people who believe the world is at their feet. Some of the people we met, and had relationships with, were single mothers, small-time drug dealers struggling to stay out of trouble, older people on benefits or minimum wage, drudging through the week and living for the weekend, in a way we would never understand. On Monday morning, while they went to work or did the school run, we stayed in bed then grumbled our way into college for a lunchtime lecture.

My parents had told me that many people go to university and then stay in that town, put down roots. Yet in Norwich my education was about London, not East Anglia. The university attracted a lot of Londoners, perhaps because it was only two and a half hours from Liverpool Street on the train; far enough to discourage your parents from coming every weekend but close enough to go home to relieve boredom, see your lover, score some familiar drugs, go to Ministry of Sound. And because the university had well-renowned English and History of Art departments it attracted posh kids. Perhaps unfairly, the posh kids from London were all dubbed 'Sloanes', a shortening of Sloane Ranger – the colloquial term for London's aristocracy that gravitated towards Chelsea, whether or not they had any attachment to that part of the city.

Some of my friends were adaptable enough to act as social bridges between us middle-class provincial types and the upper classes. Dance music and drugs was the thread that linked us, and one got the sense that reinvention at university wasn't only for middle-class kids, it was also for public schoolboys and girls who wanted a different experience. And so I found that I knew people whose parents lived in big houses in Notting Hill, who went to Marlborough College, who were part of the Nigerian Royal Family. These were very different posh kids to the ones who had so annoyed my friends and I in Henley. They didn't play rugby or hockey, they didn't wear pink polo shirts with their collars turned up, nor did they think boat shoes were cool.

I detected, or I attached, a bohemian side to these new circles of friends. There was less of a sense of rebellion about them than my friends from Henley because, well, when you're confident of your place in society, why rebel? Just have fun for three years in this funny little backwater then go back to London. Some had parents who were actors, novelists, television presenters. Perhaps because of that easy sense of entitlement, they seemed able to shape-shift between social groups. We middle-class kids defined ourselves in terms of the music we listened to in an incredibly narrow way; I was into dance music, but specifically jungle. Not techno or house or garage, just jungle. These aristocratic kids, however, floated between groups with an enviable devil-may-care attitude.

I became friends with several girls who were all slightly older and considerably posher than me. Of course, I was slightly in love with them all, but never seriously entertained the idea of a relationship. It was enough to spend time with them, listen to dub and reggae and rare groove, absorb the easy, languid confidence with which they approached their time at university. Invoking the spirit of Murakami's *Norwegian Wood*, in which the narrator hears the Beatles' song and is transported to his transformative years in college in Tokyo, if I had to select a song that does the same for me, it would be 'I Am the Black Gold of the Sun' by Rotary Connection. This 1971 slice of psychedelic soul was unlike anything I'd heard before and seemed to encapsulate a more sophisticated, cosmopolitan world, one that I associated with Portobello Road Market, Notting Hill Carnival, stoned posh kids with trust funds, rock and roll weekends in the English countryside. The music was uplifting and expansive, very different to the angry depressive guitar bands I'd been listening to only months earlier.

When the social narrowing of the second year took place, I lost touch with some of these friends. For the girls I'm sure I was never more than a mildly interesting small planet on a very distant orbit around their lives, yet for me it was an education in the world of privilege. I envied their sense of connection and entitlement. This was before I read *Brideshead Revisited*.

There was one girl for whom I had an on-off crush throughout those three years. It was on-off principally because this girl dipped in and out of view. Sometimes she would appear at the Student Union, drink and dance with the rest of us, but then disappear for a couple of weeks. I never figured out where she lived and suspected that it was probably not one of the shabby Victorian terraced houses in Norwich's Golden Triangle that the rest of us inhabited. Everyone played it very cool around her, and her style was as understated as you would expect from someone of her status (she drove a battered dark blue VW Golf), but still there were whispers… she's an *Astor*.

Mine was quite a half-hearted crush in the sense that I never expected it to go anywhere, and nor did that cause me any torment. I simply enjoyed my worship from afar, safe in the knowledge that I'd never have to experience the stress of trying to impress her. I never even spoke to her during those three years. A female friend once asked me what type of girls I liked. 'Well, like Polly Astor, I suppose,' I replied. My friend laughed so I hastened to explain – petite, brunette, pretty, someone with their own sense of style. Of course the fabulous wealth didn't interest me.

Cycling dropped out of my life entirely. I went for weeks on end without touching the bike, and without even missing it. Too busy catching up on all the fun things I'd missed out on in my earlier teenage years, I convinced myself that the landscape was too flat and boring for cycling (20 years later, I visited Norfolk with my family and discovered the county's abundance of quiet lanes that roll delicately between fields under panoramic skies). I didn't tell any of my new friends that I was a cyclist. They would have been baffled by it, and I thought that would mark me out as being clueless about the music and drugs scene we were all swimming in. I later found out that they'd guessed I was clueless anyway, it being hard to bluff your way consistently.

Throughout university my horizons were broadened, but through people rather than landscape. Occasionally, on a late-night drive to a rave, I would turn my reddened eyes to the land sliding past on the other side of the car window and make a connection to all those hours spent on my bike: the same place, different ways of looking at it.

There was still a sense of a secret landscape. We travelled at night, in convoys, our destination a mystery to us, hoping to find a gathering of our tribe. Often, because organisers needed a large empty building, illegal raves were held in disused industrial warehouses. While Castlemorton and Otterbourne were made special because there was earth beneath your trainers and sky above your head, more often you danced on a concrete floor strewn with rubbish, worrying about whether the structure above your head would withstand the assault of 300 decibels of bass. If I have one image, a kind of generic film clip in my head, of those rave years, it's stumbling out of a warehouse into the dawn light, blinking against the sun, aching and plastered in sweat, breathing in the fresh air, looking at the sparkling dew on the grass and shaking hands goodbye with the strangers I'd just spent seven hours with.

It's easy to make fun of the nineties rave scene. All the gurning, the floppy hair, baggy trousers and crazy dancing. It was so different from every music movement before it, not least because it wasn't about sex. No one went to a rave looking to find a partner; it was hedonism, escapism, pure immersion in sound. The drugs erased your inhibitions, so you talked to strangers, hugged them, shared your cigarettes and water with them. It was a collective experience, and after all my years of solitary cycling, this was a revelation.

Finally, though, the comedown became too heavy. This world grew too claustrophobic. Its pioneering and free spirit was quickly squashed by those who sought to make money and by the government, so alarmed at these incomprehensible sights that they passed a law specifically targeting music that featured repetitive beats. The police now had the power to break up impromptu, unlicensed parties.

I used to think I was such a rebel. Because I took drugs, dodged the police, danced all night. But in truth, this period was just a correction. Before that summer of 1992 my life had been dominated by cycling. Its grip on my psyche had been total. I perceived the world through the filter of knowing I was a racing cyclist. The world was split into two camps – things that made you go faster and – much bigger – things that made you go slower. An unhealthy obsession, because it isolated me. Even when I had teammates to ride with, we talked only of road race courses, training strategies, equipment.

Cycling had once been an escape, but even the methods by which we escape can imprison us. When I left university I was untethered, floating free, ready for the next wind to pull at my heart.

Symbols

It was an odd way to start, almost embarrassing. It was the autumn of 1995, six months or so after I'd graduated, and after a brief and financially catastrophic bid to move to London, I was back at my parents' house and unemployed. Mid-afternoon, I was sitting in a rocking chair in the bay window of the living room, reading *American Psycho*. The house was otherwise empty. I was supposed to be job-hunting but the inspired lunacy of Bret Easton Ellis was much more tempting.

It was the first novel I'd read in years (I'd studied Politics at university and even for that had done the minimum possible reading). A friend had recommended it because I had developed a taste for designer menswear and, well, so too did the book's psychotic and murderous main character, Patrick Bateman. I suspect my friend understood the caustic irony that Easton Ellis was applying to Bateman's materialistic world and was gently taking the piss out of me.

Perhaps I needed to escape into a fully realised other world, no matter how nightmarish. From the start I was gripped. What surprised me was that fiction could go into these sorts of places. I'd never studied literature to any great depth but had still managed to pick up the preconception that literature meant the Canon, which meant Austen and Shakespeare and Dickens and all the rest, and until you'd read the classics, you weren't allowed to progress to anything more relevant to your own life. And yet here I was reading about Giorgio Armani suits, prostitutes, business card envy, bloody chainsaws and the difficulty of getting a table at New York's hottest restaurant, and no one was stopping me. As I got further in, one thought bounced up and down in my brain: *I can do this*.

When I did sit down to write, a few days later, my lack of reading was a huge benefit. I had very little conception of what constituted good writing so I had no self-imposed barriers. Confidence, arrogance, hubris – I had those. Rather than agonising over every sentence, and comparing my own work to that of great writers, I simply pushed on. Naïve self-belief, very useful for getting stuff done. By the time I realised I wasn't as brilliant as I thought I was, I was already well down the road. I'd entered the race and done some training. May as well keep going, start reading, start learning.

That was 22 years ago.

To describe that moment when I first thought *I can do this* the word revelation feels rather overblown, too loaded with religious portent. Yet I did feel that something had been revealed, something about my identity, and about my future.

It takes some nerve to say I AM A WRITER, even to yourself. But it felt like it fitted. Everything before was preparation. Writing would help me make sense of a world I found baffling, and it would be my voice. Being diffident and inarticulate wasn't a problem when I had another way to speak.

I got a job. Moved out of my parents' house. Met the girl who would later become my wife. We built a life together that included my regular disappearance to my desk. She accepted that I was a writer, had faith in me, absorbed my fluctuating moods and I've never adequately thanked her for that.

Page after page, the joy of a rising word count.

We did things arse about tit. While most of my friends from university were living in London in shared houses, drinking in Shoreditch and going clubbing in the West End, we lived in rural Buckinghamshire, then Hertfordshire. Every day I commuted by train to my job in central London, using the hour journey to read, write and edit. And at weekends I rode my bike.

Getting back on my bike after a break of more than four years was awkward, frustrating. My body's mechanics seemed to have changed. The bike was a friend I'd neglected for so long they'd given up on me, then I'd rather sheepishly asked them out for a drink. The bike hadn't changed: it held true to its form and purpose, as stiff and fast as ever before. But now my body couldn't easily meld to its shape – the bars felt too low, the seat too high, the gears were ruthlessly racy.

The fitness I'd always taken for granted was gone, replaced with a sadly frequent downward shifting through the gears to find a rhythm I could maintain. I looked the part – I've always had good clothing – but I had no flow. Everything conspired against me: bike, road, wind, hills. And I was alone. Without riding partners, without the loose social network that coagulates around races. During the working week I left the house at seven and returned at seven, leaving little time for cycling, and riding only at weekends isn't enough to maintain any decent level of fitness. So my rides tended to be modest affairs, 20 or 30 miles, pre-planned so as to control the amount of climbing.

I wasn't sure why I was riding. It wasn't training for a race, it wasn't to get fit for its own sake – I had no interest in that. And yet still every weekend I went out for a spin. There was something deep in me that needed the bike, just as I needed to put words on the page. I didn't connect the two, but with the benefit of hindsight

I can. Because all cyclists, whether they admit it or not, are voyeurs.

Tring! Say it twice in a high-pitched voice. Tring, tring! The village in which we bought our first home was remarkably similar to the one in which I grew up and accordingly I felt an unconditional warmth for it. Tring sat 15 miles further north, at the foot of the same line of Chiltern Hills as Watlington. There was the same picturesque High Street, replete with pubs and newsagents and bad coffee, and on the edge of the village there were the same modern housing estates, some prettier than others. To the north-west Tring is hemmed in by the Icknield Way, a B-road that runs from Watlington along the foot of the hills through Bledlow, Princes Risborough, Wendover, past Tring and on towards Ivinghoe and Dunstable. Our house was tiny and cute and as soon as you walked out of the front door you came to the Icknield Way, beyond which was the Vale of Aylesbury.

I didn't hate my job, nor did I particularly mind commuting (I was getting a lot of reading done), but there is a curious futility to spending your working week at something completely separate from what you believe you should be doing with your life. I was a writer, everything else was a bullshit waste of time, so Sunday afternoons were always imbued with their own special sort of melancholy. And what better to do with melancholy than take it to the hills?

Just outside Tring there is a lane that runs down through woods to the train station – scene of Monday-morning bleariness – and out into a soft green basin of fields. Beyond the railway bridge the road has a set of perfect curves, a dip in which I gathered speed, a rise over which I could sprint. Exhilaration, sensation, freedom all compressed into half a mile. On summer evenings the low sun set the fields ablaze, warmed my calves and the back of my neck. The lane dropped through Aldbury, like Hambleden a village where time stopped in the 1950s, then slammed this speeding, joyful cyclist into a wall of reality – a steep climb out of the valley through murky beech woods. Tom's Hill. Yet even here there was some pleasure; near the top the road swivelled around a hairpin bend as shapely as any in the Alps. Kick into it, lean through it, enjoy the pain. The top's not far away.

From the top of this climb the road runs along a ridge, wide and straight, a few big houses set back in the woods, room enough for cars to give you a wide berth. Feeling more supple now, on this late October Sunday afternoon my anger at the prospect of Monday morning absorbed by the hill, I shift into the big chainring and bend my head down. And despite my lack of fitness I feel something of my old racing self, that hunger for speed and fluidity, the obliteration of everything other than the bike and the road.

At Ringshall, amid a cluster of farmworkers' cottages, I swing left. A change of rhythm as I begin the steady climb towards Ivinghoe Beacon. A few cars still parked in the National Trust car parks, pheasants darting into the hedgerow, churned-up tracks leading away into Dockey Wood, thick with autumnal russet and damson colours. The road surface now is lumpy. As if the gradient isn't enough, in wet weather several little streams flow down towards you. On a sunny evening the contours of the tarmac shine hypnotically.

The top of the climb is marked by a cattle grid, which also lets you know you are entering the National Trust land around Ivinghoe Beacon. Fields are replaced by open grassland and gorse. Fences and hedges disappear, and for a few seconds you have a clear view to the north. You fancy that you can see deep into the heart of England, to the Fens around Cambridge and Peterborough, even to Sherwood Forest. In reality, even seeing as far as the unnerving grids of Milton Keynes is a stretch.

Into the shadow of a wedge of beech trees. Beyond them, barely visible as you fly by, the fat mounds of Ivinghoe Beacon rise to meet the sky. Paul Nash came here in 1929 with his sketchbook and made some drawings that would become *Wood on the Downs*. It is an extraordinary painting, simultaneously expressive and austere, its landscape devoid of human figures yet showing the chalk curves that climb to the ancient hillfort on the Beacon Hill. This is the conclusion of the Ridgeway Path that starts in Wiltshire, the land so celebrated by Richard Jefferies, crosses my beloved Berkshire Downs then hurdles the Thames at Streatley and passes Watlington, before arriving here at the northern tip of the Chilterns. Beneath the trees is the road on which I'm descending, which Nash climbed in a friend's car, the tarmac portrayed in a pearly white. Like Ravilious, and much later David Hockney, with his watercolours of the Yorkshire Wolds, roads are part of Nash's landscapes.

Flashing out of the trees, fingers touching the brake levers, eyes quickly adjusting to rapid changes in light, I descend past yet another car park, past the wooden signs marking the Ridgeway trail, which ends at Ivinghoe Beacon, and around a tight left-hand bend always scattered with lumps of chalk. Briefly I'm facing west and the sinking sun blinds me, then I swing back to the north and across an open hillside.

I've turned for home now and that sense of adventure that comes with heading out into the hills, no matter how familiar they are, is dimmed. The landscape for the remainder of the ride is more mundane, save for the occasional huddle of Black Poplars, a huge and scruffily lovable tree that is one of Britain's rarest. The Vale of

Aylesbury is one of the few places where it still prospers. I hop between small villages, none particularly remarkable. And yet there is always something to watch.

This is the cyclist's secret. Riding through a village, he keeps his head up, ostensibly to stay safe, but really because there's a whole range of quirks of human life to be witnessed. Children playing in the garden while their parents sit drinking around a smoking barbecue, wedding parties spilling onto the street, cars parked in a secluded spot with misted-up windows, old ladies attending to the roses in front of their bungalows, teenagers waiting for the bus into town, exasperated mothers trying to negotiate with screaming toddlers. On weekends, the cyclist sees the little routines of country life – the washing of cars, mowing of lawns, cake sales at the church on a Saturday morning, bumping into one's neighbours at the village shop and stopping for a gossip.

On weekdays, if I was lucky enough to be out riding instead of being at work, these places had a very different feel. While innocent exuberance came from school playgrounds, village streets were quiet, driveways empty, churches locked. Even the prettiest village can feel eerie on a grey Thursday afternoon in November. Perhaps I'd been reading too much John Updike, with all his tales of suburban wife-swapping and quiet desperation behind twitching curtains, but I began to imagine what kind of lives lay beyond the front doors of mundane new-build houses in the Hertfordshire countryside. If we know that subversion, perversion and rebellion are integral to British suburban life, surely that could extend to villages, which are little more than marooned suburbs? After all, dramas like *Inspector Morse* are founded on the premise of violent passions running skin-deep beneath respectable provincial life.

Once, riding through the small town of Thame in a thin but persistent rain, I passed a man sitting on a bench, wearing a suit, staring into nothing, getting slowly soaked. What trauma was he contemplating? How much darkness was suffocating him? On seeing a car parked in a remote spot, there is a moment when I wonder if I'm about to stumble into a tragedy. Almost against my better judgement, my eyes are drawn to the exhaust pipe. No, no length of rubber tubing curling to a window. Thank God!

Because I was able to ride through this quietly prim landscape with no thought of getting fit, with no race to worry about, I could tilt my head up just a fraction and look at the world around me. I knew, from reading Updike and Cheever and others, that great literature often portrayed lives that were outwardly very ordinary. Why couldn't I do the same? If only I could pierce, imaginatively, the bubble surrounding the lives of the people who lived in these villages.

There is an Oxfordshire town called Wallingford, six miles to the west of Watlington, that is like a reflection of Henley, only quieter and less affluent. It too sits on the Thames and has a quaint centre that seems to be designed around a branch of Waitrose. My parents almost bought a house there when they were looking to move from Watlington, and only the fluke last-minute discovery of the house in Henley that was to become our home stopped us living in Wallingford. For that reason I've always been rather fond of the place. It's like the parallel existence I could have had.

In my early thirties I wrote a novel called *The Rebels*, though I always thought of it as *The Wallingford Novel*. That label implied to me a story about quiet lives, slowly disintegrating, set against the backdrop of the landscape in which I'd grown up. The protagonist, Bernard, was my alter ego. A librarian, he discovered his wife cheating on him, and then embarked on a mission to free the Oxfordshire Library Service from the tyranny of his boss.

I know.

In my defence, it was supposed to be funny. And it had its moments. But a novel needs more than some good moments. When my wife read it, she was dismayed. The characters were clichéd, cardboard cut-outs. I could see her thinking of all the hours I'd spent crafting it, all the hope I'd loaded onto this vessel, which, when put to sea, would surely sink. And I knew her reaction was right. Even as I was writing it, I'd known that my *Wallingford Novel* was ill-conceived. I thought I'd be able to fill the vacuum where characters should be with a facetious wit, ideas about politics, and a fair helping of graphic sex. Naturally, I was wrong, and the rejection letters told me so. Nothing can replace character.

I was 10 years older, but I'd made the same mistake as when I'd peered into the grounds of AWE Aldermaston and tried to concoct a story. This time the place that inspired me was less secretive, but in a way it was just as mysterious. I was on the outside, looking in. Pass through a place and you may see things that fascinate you, intrigue you and fire your imagination. But this is not the same as *knowing* something, and for a novelist, knowing is more important than imagining. I thought I could take a place as a starting point and imagine the lives that inhabited that place. What I'd failed to understand is that all those chroniclers of suburban woe, Updike et al., *knew* their characters. In many cases they based them upon real people. My stories didn't work because I hadn't made that connection. In my ambitious rush to get published I tried to design books, rather than let them grow naturally from people. All of which may sound like I'm trying to blame cycling for my failure as a novelist. I'm not – obviously the failure is all mine. Cycling helped me to discover how stories link to landscape, how the natural world can hold secrets, how a sense of the mystical can grow from the physical space around us. My failure was in becoming too dependent on this sense of place, and not investigating people as much as places.

Ironically, when each book was finished, and rejected, I took solace from the very thing that arguably caused my problems – the countryside. The nature of literary rejection is a slow and painful death. At first, though, there is excitement and wild hope. The work is finished, time to send it off, to lay claim to your position in the literary world. Surreptitiously, I would stay a little later in the office, until most of my colleagues had gone home, then bring up my novel, send the first three chapters to print and dash round to the printer. Fortunately, most printers spew their pages face down. There I would stand, one hand protectively on the rumbling machine, hoping that no one of any hierarchical significance would come round to collect their single – but highly confidential and tremendously important – piece of A4. With my slice of literary genius, warm as freshly baked bread, safe in my hands, I would slip it into an envelope, slide in my carefully composed covering letter and write on the front the name and address of the lucky literary agent. Names more likely to be Arabella, Poppy or Henry than Tracy or Darren.

Then the wait. As soon as I could reasonably expect the Post Office to have delivered my manuscript I began expecting *that* phone call. The anticipation was intense and delicious, like waiting for your girlfriend to ring when you're 14 years old. Back then, before mobile phones, I never actually waited beside the phone but I certainly strolled casually past it many times to check it was fully functional. Just as, waiting for an agent to call, I ensure my mobile has battery and signal.

Gradually the intensity fades. Of course, you tell yourself, they're busy people and the slush pile isn't their top priority. Still, in less rational moments you can't help imagining them picking up your manuscript, starting to read, and their eyes widening at the sheer luminous beauty of what's in their hands. The cup of coffee beside them goes cold; they ignore the phone ringing. Nothing else matters but this novel by Paul Maunder.

It didn't happen.

As the rejection letters popped through the letterbox, often months after I sent off the manuscript, I recalibrated. A letter with a few encouraging comments became a success. I started sending the book to less prestigious agencies in the hope that they had lower standards than the superstar agents. Of course they didn't. I sent the book to any publisher who was foolish enough to say on their website, we accept unsolicited manuscripts.

Was I demoralised? Yes, but an unpublished book dies very slowly. It can take years, and a small fortune in postage. Until you get to the last agent or publisher on your list, there's always hope. Stories abound of famous books being rejected right across town, then finding a lifeline from one person with vision.

Like most writers just starting out, I consumed with voracious hunger any book or article about *being a writer*. From the *Paris Review* interviews to Ted Hughes' book on the craft of poetry, *Poetry in the Making*, to David Lodge's *Art of Fiction*, James Wood's *How Fiction Works* and many more, I read anything I could that would improve my craft. A byproduct of which was that I absorbed a lot of messages about the tenacity of writers. Don't give up. Keep going. Just get to the end. These were common exhortations. Most relevant – finish one book, start the next book the following day. I realised that, for me, writing wasn't something I could give up: it was part of my DNA. So was cycling, but there was no longer any chance of cycling bringing me fame and bucketloads of money, so it seemed less pressing.

The book that expresses best how I feel about writing is Michael Chabon's *Wonder Boys*, a gentle comedy of despair in which over the course of a single disastrous weekend a middle-aged writer's life and career falls apart. The writer, played pitch-perfect by Michael Douglas in the film adaptation, is struggling to follow the huge, reputation-establishing book he had written many years before. When his wife leaves him, and his lover tells him she's pregnant, he's forced to confront some realities – that his current book is unfit for publication, that he wants a family with his lover, that he probably smokes too much weed. Along the way we see a man whose whole identity is wrapped up with being a writer. He describes it as an illness, an affliction. Throughout the story there is the sense that everyone around him forgives his bumbling, deluded, at times immature behaviour simply because he once wrote a brilliant book, and he forgives himself for the same reason. For a writer everything is research, everything is material. Even making such a mess of your life that it hurts other people.

I can only hope that I'm neither making a mess of my life nor hurting other people, yet I do feel that part of being a writer is allowing yourself freedom to follow your heart. Which is easier said than done. Sticking out of my mind at this point is a fact I picked up many years ago: the author Nicola Barker, perhaps Britain's most innovative and daring writer, loved watching *Big Brother*. This wasn't in the first years when everyone loved watching it, but later, once the novelty had worn off. At first I was a little shocked – it seemed such a clash of high and low culture. That's precisely the point, of course: a writer looks for truth and has to be open-minded enough to find it anywhere.

In his book about Marcel Proust, *How Proust Can Change Your Life*, Alain de Botton wrote about the great Frenchman's wayward cultural habits, which included a thorough daily reading of *Le Figaro*, particularly the News in Brief section, a breezy summary of the various tragedies of Parisian life that might spark a flame in Proust's imagination. Proust claimed too to favour terrible provincial theatre over the slick productions of central Paris, because the former were more likely to evoke reminiscences and ideas.

The climb up to Ivinghoe Beacon is a smooth lane hugging the hillside. On the left is a steep bank of chalky grass populated by sheep, to the right a few gorse bushes, then open space, the Vale of Aylesbury laid out. Hawks and red kites hang in the warm air currents. My wheels spin past the rabbit holes they are watching. It's the kind of climb where you have to select a rhythm, based on a gear, and then hold true to that rhythm even if it puts you in trouble. Even if your body goes into debt, hold to the rhythm and you might just make it to that next bend, after which the gradient slackens, doesn't it?

Purge your body. Put everything through the bike. Let the anger flow into the pedals. All those bastards who rejected you. No, this isn't really anger aimed at them, it's aimed at yourself, for fucking the book up. For not thinking enough, not reading enough. Another chance blown. And how long will it be before you have another warm finished manuscript in your hand?

You're a writer, because you write, and you have no choice in the matter. But if no fucker reads it, what's the point?

Streets

There is a curious melancholy about an empty office at Christmas. The half-hearted decorations, the tubs of chocolates plundered between meetings but now awaiting intrepid mice, greetings cards bearing snowy scenes toppled beside a computer someone has forgotten to switch off. Yet all this is behind me as I stand at the plate-glass window looking out across London. I'm encased in glass, steel and concrete and the silence is disconcertingly complete. Only here, insulated from the world, does one experience silence. In the natural world there is always a sound; even the most desolate moorland has the sighing wind. It's the Friday afternoon before Christmas and the last of my colleagues left 20 minutes ago, issuing the usual cheery admonishment: 'Don't stay too late.'

I'm standing close enough to the window that there is no reflected image of the brightly lit office, but not too close because the glass has two long cracks in it. The maintenance team has put small red stickers at the tips of each crack so they can see if the fissure is creeping along the glass. We're assured a replacement pane is on order and if the cracks grow enough to threaten the integrity of the window we'll be moved to a different office. I've been advising my colleagues that if things get too much they could run headlong at that window and plunge to a spectacular death. The first time I said it I got laughter, the second time nervous smiles, the third time an array of frowns. They need not worry about me making a smash for eternity. I'm not going to end up lying in a crumpled heap outside the loading bay – I know a better way to escape.

It is midwinter, almost precisely, so this teatime darkness is dense. Of course London bristles at such an imposition. This is a city with attitude, twinned with New York in its sardonic belligerence. Its northerly latitude – easy to forget that Oxford Street, if extended along some retail ley line, would run through the heart of Kiev to the east and Calgary to the west – may condemn London to wintry darkness but the city can still feel grumpy about it. After all, it only recently shrugged off those deadly pea-soupers. It's a city that prefers moaning about the heat of midsummer.

Beyond the back streets of Victoria, lit by the sodium fizz of streetlights, I can see Pimlico, Lambeth and the sorry monument that is Battersea Power Station. Never was there an iconic building more perplexing. Years, decades, of redevelopment schemes have risen and fallen, dashed by lack of finance and imagination, and by the sheer bloody awkwardness of the building's shape. The scheme that has finally been agreed upon, and is under construction on this December evening, is an unlikely combination of luxury apartments and the new American Embassy. The latter is wedged between the west side of the power station and the train tracks running into Victoria station. This huge glass edifice overlooks Battersea Dogs Home; one imagines US spies standing at their own window, as I'm doing now, gazing lovingly at some deranged Red Setter.

Looking further still, the darkness thickens around the suburbs of South London. Denmark Hill, Brixton, Dulwich… The eye is drawn upwards to Crystal Palace with its glowing tower. For a cyclist marooned in a central London office, the tower acts like a harbour lighthouse, beckoning one to safety. For beyond that hill lie the lanes that run out of the city into Kent, into the North Downs, a landscape that feels luxurious in comparison to the dreary sprawl that precedes it.

On leaving the office the cyclist-commuter gets a shock to the system. There's the blast of cold air, the sting of raindrops, the damp fabric of mist. After the stale sleepy comforts of the office the effect is energising.

Yes, I'm alive!

Click. Since the invention of clipless pedals in the mid-eighties, the sound of a cleated cycling shoe clipping into position has become, for me at least, a significant sound. In physical terms it means that one's foot is now locked into the pedal, that one is committed to forward motion. Psychologically, the sound is a statement of intent. Registering with the cyclist just below the level of the conscious mind, that click implies a certain degree of seriousness, awareness of the effort to come, and membership of the fraternity of the road. Clicking in is a much sharper and more satisfying sound than the dull clunk when one twists one's foot out. In other words, setting off sounds a lot better than stopping. Just as car manufacturers put a great deal of effort into the satisfying thunk of a car door shutting, I suspect pedal manufacturers understand the sensory power of their product.

The first few pedal strokes are both energising and appalling – my legs are so stiff. I zip through the back streets of Pimlico, taking a series of right and left turns as fast as I can, then merge with the buses and taxis of Horseferry Road. Over Lambeth Bridge, with only a glance paid to the black river – bridges and their junctions are dangerous places, you can't afford to be distracted. Down Lambeth Road, whose slight downhill gradient and width allows me to build up speed.

Riding at 25 miles an hour through London at night takes a bit of nerve. You must be tuned in to the traffic in front and behind you, and aware of all the side streets that could send a car into your path. You have to be confident in your ability to react and evade. To anticipate what drivers are going to do – never easy – and plan your channels so as to avoid them. And that's what they feel like: channels. The city is the Death Star in *Star Wars* and there is only one tiny way through it that will deliver you safely to your destination. Amid the channel is a mess of traffic and street furniture and traffic lights. The channel is constantly shifting; you are always thinking five seconds ahead. Looking for clues as to people's intentions – flashing indicator lights, obviously, but also the angle of the vehicle, where the driver is looking, where a passenger is pointing. Filter out everything else, just focus on the things that could kill you.

It's a computer game. Immersive, essential. Is that sweat lining my helmet, or adrenaline? For cycle couriers it's their daily work. They might cover 100 miles a day in these crazy, dangerous streets. When a bunch of cyclists stops at a red light in central London, the courier is the one at the front, staying clipped in and rocking gently backwards and forwards on their fixed gear, bum raised off the saddle and front wheel angled to one side. This balancing trickery, plus the bag and the radio, mark them out from us commuters. The couriers work on the streets. If ever I manage a moment of skill, I'm overjoyed. Couriers seek out such moments hour after hour. They are grizzled, lean and uncompromising. There is an element of the extreme sport about what they do, it's Parkour on bikes. While I have a personal rule never to touch vehicles (at least, not deliberately), I've seen couriers holding on to the backs of lorries, grabbing buses, grazing their handlebars against cars as they squeeze through tiny gaps. Most couriers ride on fixed gears because constantly pedalling encourages more fluidity, and the lack of gears to get grotty means less bike cleaning. Anticipation is essential – if you can see problems ahead and take evasive action, you will maintain momentum. I can understand this. Having to brake is frustrating because it kills all your hard-earned speed and means having to churn over the cranks to get back up to speed. If cycling is like flying, braking is akin to a bird falling like a stone, its wings inert, then having to work doubly hard to regain altitude.

Sometimes you cannot avoid slamming your brakes on to avoid a car that turns across your path, or a London taxi passenger opening their door into the road. Usually, though, you can see ahead what's going to stop you and take action to avoid stopping altogether. Even if you are barely going at walking pace, it's better not to have to touch the road, better to keep moving. So begins the game.

Known to all cycle commuters, the game involves trying to beat as many other commuters as possible. Going fast in a straight line is only a small element of the game, which means that anyone can take part. Choosing your route through stationary traffic, timing a mad lunge at some traffic lights, shortcuts through housing estates, diving boldly into the melee of a roundabout – it's all in the game. Because I'm vain enough to wear full cycling kit for my commute I'm probably considered a high-value target for other players. And many times I've overtaken someone on a crusty old mountain bike on open road, come to a halt at some lights, only for them to go shooting past just as the lights turn yellow and I'm struggling to clip into my pedals.

Since 2008 the game has been codified. In an online forum a cycle commuter wrote: 'It's not a race, I'm just riding to work.' From the ultra-marathon of a discussion thread that ensued, an online game was created entitled SCR, or Silly Commuter Racing. The rules are simple: you start with an FCN (Food Chain Number), the lower the better, based on what bike you're riding, what you're wearing and what accessories you sport. Based on my road bike, Lycra clothing and clipless pedals, I have an FCN of five – pretty low, and if I ever shave off my beard (I won't), it would drop to four. Out on the road the aim is to overtake riders with a lower FCN than you, which means I'm on the lookout for equally vain but slower riders, ideally clean-shaven. The SCR has no prizes other than bragging rights on social media.

My commute into London has been exactly the same for five years now, a deliberate decision to minimise the unexpected. Some days everything goes right and I have a flowing ride into town. Couriers may know the streets of London intimately, they may have a feel for road surface, drain covers and traffic light sequences, but they can never entirely predict the traffic. We're both searching for the same thing – that perfect, flowing ride, a state of Zen.

In his book *Cyclogeography: Journeys of a London Bicycle Courier*, Jon Day writes about his time working the capital's streets, and the love for cycling culture that grew from the experience. The title of his book, of course, is a play on Psychogeography, a term that acts as a kind of loose-stringed net for a range of ideas associated with urbanism, walking and radical politics.

In recent years psychogeography has been developed by writers, artists and thinkers who have tended to focus on London, and in particular on the city's liminal spaces, the gaps and edges that most of us don't notice. The writer Will Self, for example, has undertaken several walks from central London to Heathrow, a journey of around 18 miles that – it's fairly safe to say – no one ever does on foot. The Heathrow Express takes 15 minutes from Paddington station. Traversing the city in this way is a subversion of the methods and routes of travel that modern society prescribes for us, so there is a thrill of rebellion about it.

The origins of psychogeography lie in subversion too. French philosopher Guy Debord, godfather of the movement, and his Situationist International friends, developed the practice of 'the drift', which meant walking through the Paris streets being guided only by instinct. No destination, no planned route, no preconceived shape. The walker, or *flâneur*, was a man of leisure, with no need to get to anywhere in particular, and his walks usually accommodated frequent stops at cafés for alcoholic refreshment. It should be noted here that the term *flâneur* historically has been applied exclusively to men; female 'streetwalkers' have had entirely different connotations. As he drifted, marvelling at the city and its inhabitants, the *flâneur* tried to remain detached, as if gazing at these sights through a shop window. The modern city was a 'spectacle', a word that for the Situationists had negative connotations – the city was the busy, beautiful face of capitalism, but it was only a thin veil, drawn over a more profound and meaningful way of living that we are not being allowed to access.

I'm a little wary of psychogeography. As a philosophical movement it is very rooted in a specific time and place – Paris in the fifties. Nothing wrong with that. Subsequent writing about the urban environment has too often been linked to psychogeography, even if the author had no intention to make a connection. So psychogeography has become shorthand for any writing about urban environments, particularly moving through urban environments.

For the cyclist in London, or practically any other city, a random drifting journey is not only pointless but dangerous too. The cyclist doesn't have to move fast but he does need to be decisive and know where he's headed. Indecision, tentative movements, cowering in the gutter can all be fatal. In the city, on a bike, there isn't much time to look up at the spectacle of postmodern capitalism and muse on what might lie beyond…

Where cycling does coincide with psychogeography is in the cyclist's ability to dissect and bisect the city. Of course this is also possible in a car, or on a bus, but only the traveller exposed to the elements can really feel the city. I think of my commute as a straight line, cutting a paper-thin channel through the city between two fixed points, and as I move along that line I can see, hear, smell a representation of every aspect of London. My line is a microcosm, and while it might not be as long or as subversive as Will Self's walk to Heathrow, it does give me something of the same experience. And I do it every day, so I see the seasons blend into each other, I see the rain and the sun on the rooftops, I see these communities going about their daily routines.

Into Southwark, past the university buildings where my father studied, on roads I used to stumble along at three in the morning after my friends and I tumbled out of the Ministry of Sound nightclub. Past a basketball court, now deserted, where on summer evenings bicycle polo is played. And then swing left into Trinity Church Square.

And breathe... This is one of the places on the commute where it feels natural to sit up, spin the pedals and look around. The square is an elegant, peaceful place. At its centre is Henry Wood Hall, once Trinity Church, converted to an orchestral venue in 1970. The tall terraced houses around the square were built at the same time, in 1826. With uniform black front doors, black-framed sash windows, black iron railings above basement windows, they make for an imposing sight. Other than the cars parked outside, one gets the impression little has changed in this street for almost 200 years. As I ride by, I catch glimpses of some of the interiors – a pale sofa, a statement lamp, floor-to-ceiling bookshelves. One house has exhibited in its window the kind of wooden hobby horse that children aren't allowed to touch for fear of getting it grubby.

If ever there was a setting for a novel, this is it. Probably a novel by Alan Hollinghurst about an influential English family. This is one of those places that has lodged in my mind as full of possibility. But I don't feel the need to attempt to conjure up a story based around these houses. I've learned my lesson. If I find myself with a story about a wealthy London family, this could be my setting, but there's nothing to be gained from forcing it.

Back into the jumble of housing estates, shops and offices. I flick the bike through some sharp bends, down the intriguingly named Wild's Rents, then come, always, to an abrupt halt at Tower Bridge Road. When it's been raining the water pools here in the gutter, just where I would usually put my foot down.

Beyond Tower Bridge Road the landscape feels subtly different. There is still the same jumble of low-cost housing and scruffy shops but now there is a more industrial feeling too. I ride down a one-way street with an art studio on the left and a small factory on the right. At the top of this street there is always a sickly smell of barbecue sauce, though I've never succeeded in working out where it comes from. On the left, young hipsters carrying portfolio folders; on the right, white vans coming and going. Further down there's a logistics depot, from where battalions of parcel vans stream out in the morning. By the time I come past in the evening the gates are locked.

Calculations. The cyclist is always making calculations. If it isn't about gearing and cadence, or watts and heart rate, it's about road surface versus safety. There are two roads I can take to progress. One has speed bumps, long strips of shattered asphalt and a lot of traffic. The other has a newly laid surface as smooth as plastic and is part-pedestrianised. An obvious choice, right?

But this second road runs through a housing estate which puts me on edge. Now I feel exposed not to the danger of being knocked off my bike but to street crime. It's absurd, and it's based on the preconceptions of a middle-class boy afraid of being bullied by the tough kids, and yet it's not entirely illogical. This is an area with high crime, and if you live in South London, your antennae twitch when you see big cars with blacked-out windows, kids on BMXs with scarves wrapped around their faces or gathered on the streets, holding cans of lager. This is not a place to stop, or dawdle. *If you puncture here*, I tell myself, *ride it flat to the main road*. The primeval fear of the woods can transfer to more urban scenes.

I feel ashamed of the way I associate crime with this place, and my assumption that I will be a target because of my shiny bike, and so I keep riding through, trying to fight my own reaction. A more charitable response might be to feel some empathy for the people who live here. This would be the reaction of a true novelist, but fear is a primal instinct, empathy a learned one.

South Bermondsey station and Ilderton Road, notorious for its history of football violence, then past Millwall's ground, The Den, and along Surrey Canal Road, where the stench from a rubbish and recycling centre blows into your face. MOT garages, a church, a patch of derelict ground, a set of railway arches.

In Deptford I ride past a theatre, through the smells of Chinese and Jamaican takeaways, alongside a monolithic new library building, through the chlorine smell of the swimming pool where my children have their lessons. There are always groups of people hanging out in the open public spaces here, drinking and smoking weed, laughing, occasionally shouting at each other. On Wednesday and Friday evenings the evidence of Deptford's idiosyncratic market is visible on the ground – ripped cardboard, cabbage leaves, mysterious bits of metal that have fallen from crowded tables of household tit-tat.

Darting away from the traffic, I freewheel down Creekside, past art galleries clad in corrugated iron, an old mill building converted to a freelance studio space. Then my secret cut-through – a bump up a kerb and into an alleyway that runs into Greenwich by way of a pedestrian bridge over Deptford Creek. The railway arches here have been filled in, creating an expansive wall space that artists regularly use for murals. Fine art and graffiti art alongside each other and doubtless the practitioners of both have a mutual respect for each other's work. One morning I came past this wall to see a new mural, a piece of street art that celebrated Deptford's diversity.

Cool, I thought.

The next morning I came past to see that another street artist had scrawled over the mural: 'Sponsored street art doesn't count.'

Oh, I thought.

I've never thought of myself as one of the dispossessed. White, male, well-educated and resolutely middle-class, I was never threatened or excluded by the system. And I never threatened the system back. Growing up in a satellite town of London, my friends and I became fascinated with the groups that were being pushed to the fringes of the city's society: the football hooligans, the anarchists, the post-punks. We procured scratchy videotapes of *The Firm*, the 1988 Alan Clarke film about football violence, listened to the Buzzcocks, and as we got older, took tentative trips into the capital by train, antennae twitching nervously for any sign of the undercurrents. This was the late eighties, when Thatcher's vision of neoliberalism was rampant. Once a year in Henley, at the Royal Regatta, we saw thousands of former public schoolboys in candy-striped blazers, school caps, white trousers, bloated and red-faced and rich, their wives in equally offensive pastel dresses and silly hats, an invasion of the wealth-snatchers. Our rebellion, such as it was, was in reaction to this sight. Perfectly normal for middle-class, comprehensive-educated kids.

The groups we romanticised, but were too scared to join, were ultimately defeated. The prevailing and all-pervasive culture of Thatcher and her antecedents pushed everything towards the market. Rebellion has softly been absorbed into advertising. The wildest elements have been commodified. Jungle music has been diluted into television advert soundtracks, even the football hooligan's casual look has been co-opted onto menswear catwalks.

Since my teenage years this attraction to rebellious groups has ebbed and flowed. At best I have flirted with the idea of actually doing something rebellious. The classic eldest child, I am far too conformist to put myself in that place. But in London I feel closer to the sources of rebellion – as well as the targets – than I ever did in rural Oxfordshire, Berkshire or Hertfordshire.

I like the sentiment of the street artist who dismissed the Deptford mural. Of course, you cannot organise street art and direct its message, much less pay for it. It has to exist on the basis of its own anarchic energy. If it has a message, it's inevitably going to be anti-establishment. The cynic might say that every anti-establishment street artist will end up working in an advertising agency, and perhaps that's true, but behind him there will be the next generation of disenfranchised youth: we need them to cause trouble.

Cranes might be a symbol of regeneration (that word that is so hard to argue against, but invariably means shopping centre), but they also mark the death of imagination. Regeneration erases the city's scruffy spaces, the cracks and corners where artists and rebels find their oxygen. There's a scene from the film *Eternal Sunshine of the Spotless Mind* when Jim Carrey's character finds that his memories are being erased. Faces go blank, a beach house where he and his girlfriend fell in love collapses. His mind is becoming spotless and, too late, he realises that a life without blemishes may be eternally sunny but is also utterly boring. In the words of The Housemartins, who wants to live somewhere it never rains?

This concreting over of London's memories is on display, as I write, in Victoria, where the monolithic 1960s office blocks, full of civil servants and asbestos, are being pulled down to make way for glass and steel edifices, a bigger Underground station and, naturally, more retail space. The old office blocks, stained externally and outdated internally, aren't much of a loss, but the collateral damage is in the side streets and alleyways that sheltered behind. Long since pushed out of central London, artists and rebels have become the prey of the property developer – finding themselves pursued from neighbourhood to neighbourhood by the spectre of gentrification (though it's also possible to see the artists as the property developer's stalking horses…). As soon as a newspaper begins extolling the coolness of a part of London, the artists know their time is numbered. Rents will rise, industrial spaces will be converted into flats.

In Deptford, one senses a more stubborn than usual resistance to the forces of regeneration, forcing the developers into neighbouring Greenwich and Lewisham, where new buildings are sprouting in every margin. Though even in Deptford there are new blocks of flats, supported – both physically and financially – by 'metro' supermarkets. On one corner, a little off my usual route, there is a new block of flats in a tasteful dark grey brick, with a pleasingly textured look. Beside it is a row of Victorian houses converted into shops, so decrepit that they look like they've been drawn by a film set designer. There's a barber's with faded black and white photographs of the 1980s model you might want to look like, a sign proclaiming 'Internet Access', and three shops with blank frosted windows. The ground floor of the new block of flats is a supermarket, its row of expansive windows covered in vinyl pictures of fruit. On a grey day the bananas are almost luminous.

On the little bridge over Deptford Creek I dodge puddles and pedestrians, think about the playwright Christopher Marlowe, who was stabbed to death in a nearby house, note the height of the creek and the industrial barges sitting in the mud. Away to the left is the Trinity Laban dance academy, a huge hangar of a building, with sharp edges and a multicoloured translucent surface whose reflection shimmers in the creek. To my left, the trains rattle into Greenwich station. Overhead and to my right, the silent flight of the Docklands Light Railway. Suspended on a slender track, driverless trains carve through the air, carrying commuters away from Canary Wharf. Against the backdrop of scruffy, loveable Deptford, and compared to the creaking traditional train network, the DLR is a flash of the future, a piece of *Blade Runner* running every day into South London.

Avoiding the nightmarish one-way system that pitches cyclists and bewildered Spanish tourists against three lanes of traffic, I cut through Greenwich residential streets. The ground rises and so does the height of the houses, and the property prices. Like their counterparts in Trinity Church Square, the wealthy homeowners of Greenwich are happy for you to look into their rooms. For me it's a welcome distraction from the gradient of Hyde Vale, the only real hill on my route. The houses whose curtains are pulled back, where soft warm light glows, are rarely messy. Sometimes I see a family eating their dinner or a lone woman staring at a laptop at the kitchen table, but usually these lit rooms are empty. They are beautiful houses but I am no longer naïve enough to believe they are beautiful lives. I ride through the cold, dark night, blinking sweat or rain from my eyes, and when I see into these houses it doesn't conjure material ambition, instead it reminds me that I am a writer and my instinct is to peer in from the outside. I have learned the lessons of the Wallingford Novel, and the Atomic Weapons Establishment – peering in isn't enough because it doesn't create character. And yet I can't help it, my nose will always be pressed to the glass.

At the time of writing this book, I've lived in London for nine years. For a long time I didn't consider myself a Londoner, because I wasn't born in the city, and came to it relatively late in life. Yet London is composed of millions of incomers, all of whom have the right to call themselves Londoners. It's only relatively recently that I've felt like a Londoner, and more specifically, felt that this is my home.

For writers, the idea of home is central to their work. A great deal of fiction connects to the writer's relationship with the place they *feel* they are from (this may not be the place they were actually born and raised). We hanker after idealised notions of our past, or we flee from haunted places; whatever the emotional angle, we need that anchor in our work. This is not only true of writers, of course: all of us like to have a sense of where we're from, it's fundamental to our identity.

A chill April day in the Easter holidays. Away with my family on a short break to Wiltshire, I manage to squeeze in a late afternoon hour's ride on my cyclo-cross bike. We're staying near Cley Hill, and once clear of my hotel and the fast-food restaurants to which it's umbilically linked, I find a bridleway that ducks under a busy main road and climbs gradually up towards the foot of the hill. A tractor is spreading muck in a field to my right. After a couple of weeks of dry weather the bridleway is baked hard and pale. The sun is beginning to melt behind the summit of the hill, with its imposing dark terraces.

Exhilarated to be out on my bike, I stamp on the pedals and swish through bends, following the bridleway towards a bluebell wood. The noise of the road behind me has faded to a low hum, the only sound other than my own breathing is the wind in the trees. The bridleway runs close to the edge of the copse, so the sunlight penetrates, dancing between the leaves and making a moving camouflage of the ground in front of me. A movement, darting away, in the periphery of my vision. I smile at my jumpiness. A fox? An escaped panther from nearby Longleat Safari Park? Or some undiscovered feral Wiltshire cat?

Coming to a five-bar gate at the top of the climb, with a field in front of me, I stop and take a drink, survey the landscape to try and work out how to get up the hill. There are no paths heading up, only away from the hill.

I have an accelerated heartbeat from the effort of riding. Nothing odd there, but I'm also in an unfamiliar state of hyper-awareness. Not tense, but absolutely absorbent to every stimulus around me, trigger-ready. Every whisper of the leaves, every rustle in the undergrowth, and the radiance of grass bathed in late sun. I'm not scared, but neither am I relaxed. I'm alone in an empty place. People are nearby – the farmer on his tractor – but they cannot see or hear me. People have been here, but only to put up barbed-wire fences and locked gates.

I realise that I don't feel at home in this place. I'm an outsider, this is not my natural habitat. I want to feel like this is where I belong, that the English countryside is my home, but I have to face the reality that this is no longer true. Perhaps I once was a country kid but now it feels strange. That eeriness is stronger now than in a deserted suburban street or a city alleyway.

I'm more on edge in the fields and woods of Wiltshire than walking through south-east London. Driving home along the A20, I see Canary Wharf standing against a blue dusk sky, giving its slow, confident blink, and I can't help but feel that this is home. London's towers… Impersonal and brutalist maybe, but beacons too, summoning the city dwellers home from their weekend adventures. 'Bless 'em,' say the skyscrapers to each other (in Cockney accents, of course), 'they've been glamping in Wiltshire. But now they just want to get back here for some decent coffee and a faster Wi-Fi connection.'

Summit

The throaty hum of a sports car cuts through the silence of the Italian Alps. The car, a bright orange Lamborghini, glides across the Dardanelli Viaduct in the Aosta Valley and begins climbing the Great St. Bernard Pass. The camera switches between wheel-height views of the road and shots of the car's driver, a stylish middle-aged man, cigarette dangling from his lips as he concentrates on throwing the vehicle through the hairpin bends. The road is otherwise empty, there are patches of snow among the rockfaces beside the road, a wistfully upbeat song plays over the opening credits, Matt Munro singing 'On Days Like These'.

We are invited to see this scene as the very expression of happiness for a middle-aged man. Driving a fast car alone through the Alps, perhaps coming from a successful business meeting or a romantic assignation – what could be better? As the driver goes from ascent to descent we see the road curling down the mountain ahead of him, every bend a promise of exhilaration. But then the music fades away and the car disappears into a pitch-black tunnel. The camera switches to the other end of the tunnel, where a large digger blocks the road. Squealing brakes, an explosion. No more stylish driver. The mangled Lamborghini is dragged out of the tunnel and dumped over the precipitous side of the road. A sharp-suited Mafia capo watches impassively, one of his henchmen hands him a bouquet to toss after the wreck.

We can interpret the opening scene of the 1969 film *The Italian Job* a couple of ways: first, be wary of mountains, and second, never cross the Mafia. When I first saw the film, aged nine, I immediately connected the two. The mountains of Italy were beautiful, sure, but the natural habitat for the Mafia, and you don't mess with those guys. Still, the landscape of this scene, and of the famously frustrating final scene, intrigued me. In the Lake District a mountain was a big wet rocky thing to grapple with – challenging, but hardly glamorous. *The Italian Job*'s opening scene showed mountains as something utterly different – a backdrop for high-adrenaline sport, thoroughly modern and macho. Driving an orange Lamborghini through the Aosta Valley was a long way from pulling your anorak out of a sodden rucksack in Borrowdale.

Once cycling took hold of my imagination, it was the road that interested me more than the car. The slender ribbon of tarmac, thrown seemingly at random over this high, inhospitable landscape, barely wide enough for two cars to pass and edged only with stone cubes. I made another, more accurate, connection – between the high mountain passes of Europe and the Tour de France. This was the sort of road I'd seen my hero Greg LeMond fly down, pursued by that grumpy Frenchman, Bernard Hinault. No construction vehicle hired by the Mafia was going to stop LeMond. And so I began a habit that has lasted well into my adult life.

Show me a panoramic view of a mountain road and I gaze into it, following the road down the mountain, describing with my eyes the line I would take through each corner. I note where I would brake, where I would pedal, where I would let the speed gather. Cycling magazines are full of such photographs, both in features and in advertisements for kit, so evidently I'm not alone in my fantasies. Whether or not I actually ever go to this place is immaterial. For someone who lives in their head, imagining themselves into a landscape is an escape, short-lived but to be savoured.

Such pictures have recently been elevated from advertising stock to art by British photographer Michael Blann. A passionate fan of road racing, and the Tour de France in particular, Blann undertook a project to photograph the great mountain passes of Europe, centring on those that have become famous in cycling culture. The resulting images, available in a glossy coffee table book called *Mountains – Epic Cycling Climbs*, reappropriate the mountains from traditional forms of cycling photography. The vistas are expansive, the landscapes daunting in their size and wildness. Roads appear in the photographs, but they are humbled, reduced to what they really are – a recent human imposition on a sublime place. Cyclists rarely appear, and if they do, they are tiny, insignificant. Seeing these famous roads – the Col d'Aubisque, the Col du Tourmalet, Alpe d'Huez – stripped of the bike racing circus is refreshing. A sense of scale is restored and the viewer is reminded that the roads themselves are accomplishments of design and engineering. In the preface, Blann says: 'I have always preferred to shoot from afar. I naturally take the viewpoint of the passive observer looking over the wider scene as it unfolds before him. This detachment encourages a sense of quietness and deep introspection, which in turn is reflected in the final image… I wanted to document the permanence of these landforms, their relative scale and their sheer presence. I wanted to capture the unique character of every mountain – the roads and man-made structures that punctuated the landscape, its vegetation and the impact of the seasons.'

Dotted throughout the images are the buildings that stand on top of some of the high passes. Hotels, visitor centres, cafés, ski stations, all distant from the camera's position. These are places of refuge in an awe-inspiring landscape, and a reminder that you'll stay safe if you follow the road. Even in the wildest places, the cyclist remains tied to civilisation.

I was fast. Seriously fast. I had a yellow Peugeot jersey, black woolly shorts and perforated leather shoes. Admittedly, I had an embarrassing handlebar bag strapped to my bike, but overall I felt and looked good. I was 11 years old and riding on the roads of my heroes. The côtes and cols of the Isère region may have been mere foothills to the professionals, but for me they embodied everything I dreamed about. I'd seen enough coverage of the Tour de France to know how you ride up these hills, how to swoop through the hairpins and blast through sleepy villages.

I was enjoying myself, though there was quite a lot of downtime. The agreement with my parents was that I would wait at the top of each hill, or at a junction. So for all my sprinting through sets of hairpins, I had to spend 20 minutes at the top waiting for my mother on her Dawes Galaxy touring bike, and my father, who had given himself the masochistic challenge of riding around the Isère on a tandem that weighed more than a nuclear submarine. He did have a stoker on the back, but she was seven years old and, being more interested in ballet than cycling, spent as much time as she could with her feet perched on the top-tube.

Nevertheless, I enjoyed those interludes waiting astride my bike in the middle of the French wilderness. The sun beat down, the verges buzzed with early summer life. Occasionally one of those vans that are unique to France – battered, grey, cute – would chug past and its driver, equally battered and grey, would peer at my jersey. Often I'd get a nod, or a raised finger, and that bolstered my opinion that I was, one day, going to win the Tour de France.

One day, at the top of a climb, I noticed a page of a newspaper, yellowed, abandoned and blown into the ditch beside the road. There was a large photo of a rider in a Renault Elf jersey. I jumped off my bike and into a ditch. Pored over the photo and the adjacent text. The fact that I didn't speak a word of French became, for the first time in my life but not the last, acutely problematic. Folded the newspaper page and tucked it inside my jersey. There then followed a general regrouping of the family peloton before a headlong plunge down to the valley. A junction.

Merde (OK, I knew some words). I stopped again.

The wait after descents wasn't so long because the gravitational forces acting upon the tandem, combined with its near-useless brakes, meant that my father had little choice but to take the descents at speed. It was also a good opportunity to take revenge on my soft-pedalling sister. She always looked terrified at the bottom. My mother held the rather odd perspective that down-hills were a good opportunity to look at the view, so she brought up the rear.

Rolling once more, I found more newspaper pages blowing across the road. I stopped, retrieved them and showed them to my father.

'Look, Stephen Roche, Eric Caritoux, Sean Kelly.'

'Must be a race on,' he replied sagely.

Our combined linguistic skills couldn't decipher any of the articles, so I pocketed the pages and we carried on our way.

It occurs to me now that my parents may have known all along that the following day we were going to happen across one of professional cycling's most intriguing and stylish events, the *Dauphiné Libéré*. If they did plan it in advance, they certainly made a good job of feigning surprise when we walked into the market square of a small town, looking for ice creams, and discovered the village du départ.

I was in heaven. Here were all the team cars – Skil, La Redoute, Panasonic, Kwantum, Renault. Rows of glittering beautiful bikes. The breathless narrative of the race announcer over the loudspeakers. For me, the only thing more evocative of a bike race than a French announcer is the sound of the musical horns they still fit in team cars. I stumbled from car to car in a state of euphoric awe. My bedroom walls were lined with photos of these riders cut out from magazines. And here they were, just lounging about in their team cars, fiddling with their kit, joking among themselves. They were real. And yet they glowed with the aura of the supernatural. The Café de Columbia team, home to the gifted climber Lucho Herrera, sat in a line on a kerb, drinking espressos. An obligation by their sponsors, I thought; this was long before my own caffeine addiction took hold. My father focused on more technical matters, shaking his head in amazement as he watched a mechanic strip down the gears on a blue Gitane.

At the Skil car we found Sean Kelly sitting in the passenger seat with the door open.

'Long one today, Sean?' ventured my father.

'Not really, 180km.'

'Christ,' muttered my father, genuinely disturbed by the answer. Perhaps he was thinking about doing 180km on the tandem.

Emboldened by our first exchange with a supernatural being, we went off in search of other English-speaking riders. Phil Anderson beamed as he had a photo taken with me. Robert Millar was quietly charming. As I squared up to have my photo taken with Stephen Roche, I told him that I wanted to be a pro when I grew up.

'That's what I said,' he smiled back, 'and look what happened to me.'

Years of rejection take their toll. For almost 20 years I'd been writing fiction, sending it off in neat little packages, waiting, waiting some more, then receiving rejection letters. Four novels, plus a couple of half-finished attempts. I felt that I was improving, that each book was better than the last. Indeed, I regularly received encouraging comments from literary agents. But I wanted a publishing contract, not just encouraging remarks.

My fourth novel took me three years to write, then another two years of editing and rewriting, 18 drafts in all, and attracted the attention of an editor at the kind of powerhouse literary imprint I'd always dreamed of. I felt like all my hard work and commitment, all those late-night and early-morning sessions, all the reading, the soft-pedalling I'd done in my day job because I was too knackered to focus, now it was all worthwhile. I wasn't particularly surprised or overjoyed by her interest, it was more a feeling of relief. Finally, I would be able to say, I am a writer, without any qualifying addendum.

She passed.

There followed a rather terse meeting with my agent. I was too good to give up, it was time to move on. And next time I had to focus on story.

When I left her central London office and walked through Soho I didn't feel despondent. Two-thirds of me felt that she was wrong, that the novel would eventually find a home, even if it wasn't a major publishing house. The other third of me thought, well, if it really is dead in the water, then I'll start the next book. I'll start it tomorrow. Fuck rejection. Keep going. Work hard. Never give up.

And that's precisely what I did. But everything I started was a version of the crippled story I'd just finished. My ideas were stale. And the prospect of another three or five years working on a novel, only to go through the same process, was thoroughly depressing. Was my life really going to slip by in chunks of three to five years, marked out with rejection letters?

Stop. Fuck it. Enjoy yourself. Give up.

Cycling saved me. More specifically, a chap called Ian.

A neighbour who earned her living as a freelance journalist told me, as we stood nursing cups of coffee in the playground one blustery Saturday morning, about how she pitched feature ideas to magazines and newspapers. A few days later, I came home from work with a slippery stack of cycling magazines.

Ian, the editor of *Rouleur* magazine, commissioned a feature on the basis of a brief email exchange, and a few weeks later I was a published writer. It was so simple. A few weeks later, I got paid.

I pitched more ideas, published more features. Expanded to an American magazine, then a Dutch magazine. Got a press card.

That's how, 30 years after seeing the race as a child, I went back to the Dauphiné to research two features. After a bumpy flight to Geneva and a third-gear crawl along the banks of Lac d'Annecy, I arrived in the town hosting the first stage, Albertville, and met up with a photographer friend for dinner.

That evening the heat turned into a fierce electrical storm. Driving out of Albertville, huge raindrops fell onto my windscreen, gathering pace until there were curtains of water falling on my little car. Grey then purple-black cloud cover rolled out above the mountains. The heavy bass of thunder, though with a crackly sharp edge to it, like rock being split from a cliff face, drowned out the Europop on my car radio (music I hate, but somehow it's impossible to turn off).

Turning out of the valley, past a cement works and lush meadows, I drove up through the forest. The small river running alongside the road looked energised by the rain. In front of my car the tarmac danced and convulsed. Beyond my frantic windscreen wipers I could see where I was going, but only just. At a lonely crossroads beside a stone bridge I checked my crumpled yellow Michelin map and turned onto a narrow road climbing steeply away from the river. Wrenching the car through hairpins awash with grit and films of rainwater, I climbed and climbed, headlights flickering yellow through the dense forest.

A ski resort in midsummer can be a strange place. Most of the lodges and hotels in Crest-Voland were shuttered, their impressive log stacks waiting for winter. The ski equipment places too. Motionless chairlifts let out a plaintive creak from time to time. Deprived of the white stuff, this place had lost its meaning. My hotel, being one of the few open in the area, was full of cyclists. Some seemed to be there for the Dauphiné, but most were there to ride the nearby famous climbs. By the time I came down for dinner the storm had swept itself away. Looking across to the peak of La Grande Balmaz and the Chaîne des Aravis stretching away beyond it, the sky still showed some bruised clouds among the drifts of blue and the low fluorescence of the evening sun.

The next day I tanked up with coffee and croissants and pulled on my cycling kit. The air was sharp and chill. It was early on a Sunday morning and outside the hotel, nothing was moving. The click of my helmet strap and the clunk of cleat into pedal were loud protests against the silence.

From the first pedal stroke I was climbing. Soon out of the village, legs complaining at being asked to work so hard, amid cow pastures, the road turned gently back and forth. No road markings, few signs. The gradient was manageable but unrelenting. As my muscles began to soften, sweat rose to my skin, then began to bead on my forehead and run down from my temples. I listened to the ebb and flow of my breathing, watched my carbon-fibre shoes bob up and down.

Climbing is fear. There's no getting away from that, whatever kind of cyclist you are, because a climb will always test you, will always find you out. The landscape dictates what kind of fear you are going to experience. British hills are generally shorter and steeper; the fear they summon is of short-term pain, of hitting a gradient that makes you wobble and weave. If you are unfit or horribly overgeared you may suffer the ultimate humiliation for a serious cyclist – having to put a foot down. On a long ride, the cyclist grows afraid of a repetition of hills. As fatigue grows, so does the dread of coming round a bend to be faced with a wall of tarmac.

Mountains, like the Col des Saisies I was tackling that morning, provoke a different kind of fear – that of the slow collapse. We grow up watching the Tour de France, noting the varying rhythms of the riders, how pure climbers vary their rhythm, while all-rounders have to stay more consistent. And we've seen many times the rider being dropped from the group of leaders. A slow, cruel death. Slipping backwards, his wheel unable to hold that in front, his shoulders bobbing, pedalling laboured. This shot is always from behind because the TV motorbike is positioned there. So we don't get to see the rider's face until the fight is lost, when the motorbike cruises past to catch back up to the group, as it does so giving the viewers a profile shot of the vanquished rider.

The longer this profile shot lasts, the more famous the rider is, and therefore the more heavy the defeat. Sometimes there is a self-conscious sideways glance, sometimes the rider cannot bear to acknowledge the camera's presence, for this side-on shot seals the lid on failure. In a moment, all hope is gone. Victory, prizes, pride – all disappearing around a bend in the road. The rider settles into a new rhythm, in a lower gear, and wishes the road would swallow him up.

The amateur riding on the same mountain pass has no wheel to cling to, no vehicles burning their clutches 10 metres behind. He has only his own calculations of speed, cadence, gears. And pain. How long can I keep this up? Will my limit come before the summit? It's not a case of evaporating strength so much as mounting distress. Your brain is telling your legs the power they need to produce, but the force required hurts, hurts a lot, and gets progressively worse. Pedalstroke after pedalstroke, pain upon pain. A water torture with drips of lactic acid. There is no relief, and the final release may be many kilometres away. It is the same principle as a sprint for the finish line or for a traffic sign – the same simple mechanics of power and momentum, but the psychology is vastly different.

The sprinter's brain is a frenzy of tactical machinations – which wheel to follow, wind direction, road surface, gradient, gear choice. The physical pain of pushing that gear hardly registers because it is so brief, and there is no choice. Once in the right position, the sprinter simply makes his bike move as fast as he can without falling off, and hopes it will be enough. There is pain, of course, but the visceral intensity of the whole experience overwhelms it. The climber, by contrast, is moving slowly. He may be climbing for many minutes, even hours. The sprinter can only measure his competitors in those final few seconds when they may or may not come past him. For the climber, the battle is psychological. He watches his fellow riders, tries to judge who is struggling and who is feeling good. And all the time he is trying to judge whether he himself is feeling good; the race is played out in the heads of the group of riders, and as the finale approaches those who are feeling good are able to start applying pressure to those who aren't.

In cycling we celebrate climbers as a unique breed. They are angels, eagles. Their talent is often referred to as God-given, the implication being that climbers are more akin to artists. Whether they like it or not, they are obliged to use that talent, they owe it to us mere mortals. And as with artists we are prepared to accept their flaws. It's the other side of their talent. Perhaps we even encourage those flaws, attempt to tease them out. Without villains, eccentrics, provocateurs, a story is dull. That is Creative Writing 101. Cycling fans, through the media, love to create a mythology around talented riders.

When I attended the residential writing course at Totleigh Barton, that rambling farmhouse tucked deep into a fold in the Devonshire land, there were two established writers presiding over us fledglings. One was the novelist Jim Crace. Having done my research, I knew that he was an avid fan of cycling, had done some cycling journalism before moving into fiction, and it didn't take long for the dinner conversation to drift that way. Naturally our conversation bored and excluded everyone else, until one of my fellow students asked, in a rather pointed tone: 'Yes, but what would you rather be – a writer or a professional cyclist?'

'A professional cyclist,' I replied without hesitation. 'But I was born with the wrong heart and lungs, so writing will have to do.'

Recently, I took up the conversation again with Crace, and asked him what he thought of our attachment to climbers.

'You only have to think about the wider, metaphorical and biographical implications of the words *ascent*, *descent* and *summit* to understand why the endurance deeds of the climbers nearly always outweigh the sporting on-the-flat deeds of the time-triallists and the sprinters,' he told me.

'To be a truly tragic grimpeur hero, a cyclist needs to confound the usual stereotypes of the sportsman. He needs to be a small, slight maverick, disdainful of his *domestiques* – not truly needing them, in fact. That's why champions like Indurain, Ullrich and Armstrong will never be included on our list. Where's the romance in the muscle men? There might have been no Tommy Simpson mythology if he'd collapsed and died on the flat. For the tragedy and the glory of his death to have great power, there had to be a mountain bearing down on him. It had to seem that landscape itself had defeated him just when it appeared that he and his bicycle were defeating it.'

As part of his 1957 book *Mythologies*, which covered topics as varied as wrestling, Billy Graham, Citroën cars and steak-frites, the French philosopher and cycling fan Roland Barthes published an essay on the Tour de France. His argument, persuasively put, was that the race closely embodied the Epic. This is a word that has become overused in the cycling world; indeed, Michael Blann's lavish photographic book of cycling vistas is subtitled *Epic Cycling Climbs*, its meaning being reduced to anything of scale or prolonged periods of racing action. Naturally Barthes uses the word correctly, outlining why the Tour is analogous to the ancient myths. Its journey is akin to the *Odyssey*, its racers are Homeric warriors.

These rare creatures, climbers, are always looking to escape, to fly above everyone else. Often they possess complicated, intense personalities. They can seem dour, unfriendly, even tending towards depression. Yet in the high mountains they come alive. They seek redemption in the solitude of altitude, victory is almost incidental.

In *Mountains of the Mind*, an exploration of man's obsession with climbing mountains, Robert Macfarlane writes of man's innate ambition to ascend: 'the equation of height with goodness is embedded in our language and consequently in the way we think. Our verb "to excel" comes from the Latin *excelsus*, meaning elevated or high. Our noun "superiority" is from the Latin comparative *superior*, meaning higher in situation, place or station. "Sublime" originally meant lofty, distinguished or raised above.'

In cycle racing, mountains are a test. Physical, moral, perhaps even spiritual. Those who pass are romanticised as heroes; those who fail are forgiven, praised for their bravery. Amateur riders from all over the world travel to the Alps and the Pyrenees to emulate the feats they have witnessed on television. Encouraged by magazine features, they want to feel the force of the wind on Mont Ventoux, the sun bouncing off the moonscape of the Col d'Izoard, the crippling gradients of the Mortirolo.

Years ago, when we watched patchy footage of the Tour de France on television, these places remained remote. Now, in a world of social media and immediate content, we are there. The remoteness has been lost. We can look at any climb on Google Street View, check its Strava numbers, and we can buy holidays to ride up it with professional-level support. Road surfaces are better than ever, bikes are lighter and more reliable, wide access to sports science is giving the average cyclist the chance to be fit enough to take the toughest climbs. The remoteness has been lost.

Yet, as Blann illustrates, these places are both bigger than cycling and wilder than the kind of landscapes most northern Europeans are accustomed to. Their emptiness can be unnerving. And their gradients are no easier for being more visible.

Most of the famous climbs of the Alps and Pyrenees are passes, taking the traveller from one valley to the next by the shortest feasible route. They may have been little more than mule tracks for several hundred years, but in the early 20th century engineers plotted roads to these high places, enabling cars to reach the previously secluded villages beyond. For cyclists these mountain passes make a rudimentary kind of sense; they are a passage from one place to another. They are an obstacle – a mighty one – but in the context of the journey, necessary.

The other category of mountain climb is the road that goes nowhere, only to the top. The top may be a sizeable ski resort, as at Luz Ardiden or Alpe d'Huez, or an inhospitable telecommunications mast, as at the summit of Mont Ventoux. It doesn't matter. Climbing this sort of mountain is an exercise in futility; the only reason can be to test oneself against the road. Psychologically, it seems to me, this futility makes dead-end climbs harder.

In the hope of creating myths as powerful as that surrounding Ventoux, other races have tried to find similar mountains. In Spain the Alto de Aitana, rising above the Costa Blanca, is sometimes referred to as Spain's Mont Ventoux. In geographical terms there are similarities. Both are formed of limestone, giving their exposed surface a glimmering shade of off-white, both stand in splendid isolation above the surrounding landscape, and both have bald summits, where the wind whips across without mercy. To give it an air of mystery, the top of the Alto de Aitana is inaccessible to the public on every other day of the year; it is occupied by a military communications station. Yet this climb doesn't live in the public consciousness the way Ventoux does, and the reason for that lies in the way the Tour de France was marketed, over 100 years ago.

After the successful, if rather chaotic, beginnings of the Tour de France in 1903, the organisers, led by Henri Desgrange, sought out ways to make the race more difficult, to place seemingly impossible tasks in front of their brave riders. The Tour was a race but it was also conceived as an experiment in human endurance. Desgrange, the editor of the newspaper *L'Auto*, wanted to astonish his readers so he took the race into the mountains. From 1910 onwards, the 325km stage from Luchon to Bayonne, passing over the cols of Peyresourde, Aspin, the Tourmalet, Soulon, Tortes and the Aubisque, became a deciding factor in the race. And *L'Auto*'s coverage set the tone for the myth-making that would become a permanent feature of the event. Desgrange and his fellow writers followed each stage by car, and afterwards wrote hyperbolic reports of the action. In *The Tour de France*, 1903–2003, a uniquely academic analysis of the event, Philippe Gaboriau describes how 'Everything tended towards the embellished, the excessive and the spontaneous. The writer, the speaker was at one with the reader. He admired just as much as the other did. In the tone of writing, a new kind of communication took shape: the live report. Nature becomes personified, cols become giants who are challenged and monsters who are defeated by mythical heroes.'

Desgrange's report of the 1911 crossing of the Galibier pass illustrates the point: 'In the history of mankind, is not the bicycle the first successful effort of intelligent beings to rid themselves of the laws of gravity? "These are eagles," Maurice Leblanc told us more than 15 years ago, and are these men of ours not winged, since they have now managed to rise to heights where eagles do not venture, and cross the highest peaks of Europe?'

The Tour de France and *L'Auto* were the perfect reciprocal marketing stratagem – each sold the other. When Mont Ventoux was introduced to the French public in 1951, the same Epic tone was applied. The bald giant was portrayed by cartoonists as a monster lying in wait for the cyclists. *L'Equipe*'s writers described the torturous mix of furnace heat, gradient and wild Mistral winds. Barthes may have linked the race and the climb to ancient mythology, but he was only building on the long-established reputation of the mountain.

On the Col des Saisies I pushed myself, trying to keep the *souplesse* in my pedalling, jumping out of the saddle on the exit from every hairpin. It was to be a short ride; no need to conserve energy. The previous day someone had said to me that this was an easy climb so I couldn't let it defeat me. As I slogged away, the sound of a car drifted up from further down the hillside; a high-powered vehicle, its engine note rising and falling as it took the bends. Louder, closer, the noise filling the mountain air. Giving me a respectfully wide berth, a red Porsche blazes past and disappears into the next bend. I'm reminded of *The Italian Job*'s opening scene. The high mountain passes of Europe, on a bright sunny day, are an incongruous place for gangsters to kill their enemies, which is why the scene is so effective. I hope the red Porsche isn't about to meet an unforgiving digger truck.

At the summit of the Col des Saisies is the village of Les Saisies, another shuttered ski resort. Cafés, shops, expansive car parks, ski lifts to take skiers up into the snow. I stop, take a drink, have a bite to eat. I've been riding for an hour, all of it uphill. As I ride back through the village to start descending the mountain I've just climbed, I see the red Porsche again. He too is turning around. The driver is a lone male, no surprise there, and he waves cheerfully at me. There is kinship in our shared enterprise – go up a mountain and then back down. We're both being as pointless as each other, so why not be happy about it?

Ascent, summit, descent. As Jim Crace implied, here is a metaphor with wide-ranging and powerful connotations. In our careers, relationships, physical well-being, we often paint the story of our lives in such terms. Those with ambition, whether empire builders, politicians or pop stars, have a rise then a fall. The loftier the ascent, the more dramatic the descent. Perhaps that's why climbing Alpine cols on bicycles appeals so much to middle-aged men; because there is an inherent sense of the mid-point in life, the bike ride is a confirmation of where they are in life, and what lies on either side.

Bikes leave no trace on the landscape, so every ride is an act of disappearance. We disappear into the countryside and our very ride disappears even as we do it. I've grown up understanding and valuing this; for me a bike ride will always be an escape, invisible to others. I ride without a GPS device and I don't use Strava, the social media app for athletes that allows you to record and share the statistics of the ride. Partly this is because I am hopeless with technology, but mainly because the statistics are always the least interesting thing about any bike ride. And yet I can understand the urge to record and share. It is an act of affirmation, a statement of vigour and adventure. Look at me out on my bike – I'm still young at heart. A softer way, perhaps, to have a mid-life crisis. Less expensive than buying a sports car and less damaging than having an affair.

The summit of the Col des Saisies is something of an anticlimax. It's the same at most mountains. There will be a sign giving the col's name and altitude, often plastered in stickers from those who wish to mark their successful climb (the stickered sign is the road cyclist's equivalent of a cairn). If you're lucky there will be somewhere to get a *café au lait*. But of course the summit as a physical place is not the point. The summit is more important as an idea in the mind of the struggling climber; the summit doesn't need to offer coffee and cake, it only needs to offer an end to the suffering. Once there the rider can take in the scenery, then begin their descent.

Here our metaphor begins to unravel. In life, falling from a position of power, prowess or achievement can only be unpleasant. In cycling, riding down a mountain is exhilarating and invigorating. The intensity sets your nerves jangling, makes you feel alive.

From Les Saisies I rode back in the direction I'd come, zipping up my jersey and taking some sips from my bottle. The road began gradually to drop, making pedalling unnecessary as my wheels hummed and the chill air swept into my face. The bends came upon me, first gentle and sweeping, then tightening up as the gradient steepened. Fingers resting on the brake levers, trying to relax, sitting back in the saddle and looking, always looking. Find the right line through the apex, how far to drift out on exit, setting yourself up for the next bend. Assessing the surface, wary of gravel, patches of water caused by a mountain stream spilling onto the tarmac.

A fast descent is a search for perfection. The rider tries to go from top to bottom with the fastest line through every bend, touching his brakes as little as possible. This is the moment to enact all those times you've gazed at photographs of mountain roads, following the bends with your eyes. As with any search for perfection, frustration is near at hand. If you are tired, mistakes will come; if the weather is a distraction, you will need to temper your speed. Get one corner wrong and you will lose your momentum for the next 10.

French writer Paul Fournel, in his collection of observations on cycling, *Velo*, observes on descending: 'To be a good descender, you've got to have a good knowledge of the road – a kind of complicity with the civil engineers, an instinctive and rapid grasp of the terrain. Every road is a design, and every descent is a design within the design. Modern roads dictate their law with blows from bulldozers and dynamite, but the older ones embrace the contours of the ground and of the mountain'.

Watching a good descender in a race on television can be breathtaking. To see the combination of courage, intelligence and technique at play, each bend taken smoothly, makes you quite jealous. On the other hand, watching a weak descender makes you grind your teeth.

Even if you take a descent relatively easy, don't attack it, your mind will be empty of everything else. Thinking is restricted to the present moment, to make this combination of road-bike-human stay in its correct configuration. For the descending cyclist, crashing is the darkness at the periphery of your mind. One does not entertain it, but it's always there. Descending requires articles of faith. First, you put faith in your own bike-handling. Second, you put faith in not having a blow-out, a rare but potentially devastating phenomenon. And lastly, you put faith in external forces staying away from you. The cyclist is always vulnerable but at 50 miles an hour to find a car in the wrong place or a cow crossing the road (a common occurrence in the Alps) is life-threatening. Risk-taking, the deliberate act of putting oneself in danger, in this case a controlled and moderate danger, has always been a feature of mountain pursuits. To a non-cyclist descending a mountain pass at 80km/h on skinny tyres and a lightweight frame, wearing only a thin layer of Lycra, probably seems as lunatic as climbing up the other side of the mountain for no obvious reason. Cyclists know that we climb to escape the mundane and to redeem ourselves. We descend simply to feel alive.

On the Col des Saisies I flew into the lower slopes, through the village of Le Planay, where speed bumps and parked cars added new dimensions of risk. Tears streamed from my eyes, my hands were beginning to ache from gripping the bars and my legs were stiffening. Near the bottom I found the left turn that would take me back up to Crest Voland, to my hotel, where a shower and coffee awaited. And as I winched myself up this unexpectedly steep final section I felt vaguely dissatisfied.

The ride had been an opportunity to explore this rarified landscape and two hours hadn't been enough to really challenge myself. There was no way I could truthfully call this ride Epic. *And perhaps*, I thought as I drove in my car back through the forest towards Albertville, *riding in a foreign place will never be as satisfying as riding at home*. That's not to be insular or to devalue the spirit of exploration, it's just that riding on foreign roads can be a dislocating affair. One engages with the land only superficially. Everything is different: the road markings, the irrigation channels to cope with spring's melting snow, the way local drivers gun their cars around switchback bends, meadows thick with wildflowers, the type of rubbish jettisoned from passing cars, the sky being reduced and intensified by the bulk of the mountains. Only a cyclist sees these differences; the car driver is too busy and too insulated; the walker avoids the road.

The cyclist riding abroad is hungry to consume these differences, indeed cannot help but absorb them. It may be a form of tourism, but it creates a genuine connection. To ride in a new place is to understand it, for how else do humans exist than on their roads?

And yet this process of absorption is only skin-deep. It will take many weeks, months and years of riding before a cyclist finely tunes to the nuances of a landscape. Until then our eyes are blunt instruments. And aesthetics are only part of the puzzle's solution. Understanding something of the history of a landscape, the layers of trauma, politics, human endeavour, is important. So too a knowledge of the people who live and work there, how they spend their weekends, how they respond to the changing seasons. The final layer is the cyclist's own personal history. Live and ride in a place for any length of time and you cannot help but imbue the landscape with an emotional power. The road is a place to empty your head, to submit your body to suffering, to take the heat out of raw emotion. The hills may cause you physical pain, but they will also absorb your emotional pain.

The landscape in which I grew up, in which I learned to be a cyclist, is not as remarkable as the Alps. It's beautiful in an understated way, we might call it quintessentially English. We may also decide to reject that term for being too reductive and too weighed down with unfortunate cultural baggage. The cyclist knows that every landscape holds surprises, secrets. To portray a landscape as belonging to one simple idea means missing out on its true, more mysterious and shifting, nature.

Another thing every cyclist knows: you never fall out of love with your home roads. They are the neural pathways in your brain, and the arteries leading to your heart.

Suburbs

A Sunday morning in February, before dawn. I'm sitting at the kitchen table, half-dressed, trying to force down a bowl of porridge. Dumped on the chair next to me is a jacket, helmet, gloves, skullcap, tools, food, money – the preparations for even a short ride in winter are laborious. Upstairs my family are asleep so everything I do has to be as quiet as possible. The kitchen window is an impenetrable black; I can see only my own reflection. No bad thing – at least there are no streaks of rain.

Once fully dressed I want to get out of the house as quickly as I can. The central heating has come on and I've got so many clothes on, it's unbearable. At a more civilised hour I would spend longer shuffling about the kitchen, drinking coffee, looking for food to put in my pockets, adjusting my clothing and fiddling with my helmet straps… I've known many cyclists who behave similarly, working themselves up to actually grabbing the bike and opening the front door. It's not nerves exactly, more like an old train building up a head of steam.

Now for the biggest challenge of the morning: closing our ancient front door. Usually it needs a hefty slam; this morning that would certainly wake up the children. Every minute that they continue sleeping is another minute less of guilt. Mornings can be easy, if no one is in a grump, if the children eat their breakfast, but they can also be a battleground. My wife has kindly given me time to ride my bike, the least I can do is avoid waking everyone up. I pull the door slowly, gently, willing the stiff lock to slide noiselessly into place. Click. I wince, but that wasn't too bad. Not moving, I listen for yelling. Silence.

Across London, across the country, middle-aged men are performing the same stealthy escape. I imagine us all carefully putting our porridge bowls in the dishwasher, slipping on our cycling shoes, pulling shut our front doors as if we are Indiana Jones facing a deadly challenge. A collective comedy routine that will give us a couple of hours on the bike.

We meet at an unlovely crossroads, just around the corner from my house. The lorries queuing at the traffic lights have likely come straight off a ferry from mainland Europe; whether by accident or design, this is a good time to drive into central London. Our scruffy neighbourhood, with its tattoo parlour, derelict pub, launderette and darkened Sainsbury's, is just another uninteresting place to drive through. Though for anyone with a sense of the invisible lines that humans have imposed on the land, this is actually a place of some significance. A mile or so to the north is Greenwich, home of the Prime Meridian, zero longitude. And that powerful yet fictional line runs right through my neighbourhood, bisecting almost exactly our local train station. This is where East and West start, but in that usual London manner we accept it with a casual sarcastic aside, don't stop to consider the historical resonance. When we go to Greenwich Park to kick a ball about with our children we're shocked to see tourists lining up to have their pictures taken standing over the line that we live with day by day.

There are five of us this morning. A minimal greeting, then we bump down from the pavement and ride, lights blinking, reflective strips flashing. We head south, following the route we always take out of the city, through sleeping suburbs: Grove Park, Sundridge Park, Bromley, Hayes. At any other time of day it's six miles of frustrating stop-start riding. The roads are clogged, which is something you can accept in central London, but out here in the suburbs I expect a flowing ride without having to stop. On Sunday mornings I get that clear run, but almost wish there was some traffic around to slow us down; this group heads off fast, there's no time for easing yourself in. My poor cold aching limbs…

The weekend escape from the city has always been a feature of cycling in Britain. The focal point of any cycling club is the Sunday morning club run that meets in a suburb and swims, a shoal of whirring fishes, out into the countryside. In industrial cities cycling clubs have always been a valve by which working-class men (sadly, it was predominantly men) let off pressure. Growing up in Glasgow, comedian Billy Connolly was a keen club cyclist in the days when dockers and factory workers would escape from the city on long, boisterous club runs. A few years later, a young Robert Millar joined them. Millar was immensely talented and driven, and though a very quiet introverted individual, he rode with the club because, well, in those days that's what you did. Club-mates remember him as mostly riding off the front of the group, and when they stopped for something to eat, he would sit apart from everyone else. Connolly later coined a phrase that perfectly captures the curious paradox of cycling as an activity for loners, undertaken in groups. 'Cyclists,' he said, 'are sociable loners.'

Our little Sunday morning group is shamefully homogenous. We're all white men around 40, with young children, living in one small middle-class enclave of South London, mostly working in creative jobs. Indeed it's the children that originally brought the group together. Toddlers have a way of creating adult networks they're not aware of. I'm on the periphery of the group because I'm terrible at getting up so early on a Sunday – or any day. But when I do manage to crawl out of bed, I enjoy the sensation of riding with other people.

Talking is a rhythm that has to fit your pedalling. Among cyclists who often ride together conversation can be spare or profuse but it always has a natural fluidity. Pedalling is adjusted to ensure the rhythm of a conversation is maintained, or the conversation is paused to allow for momentary changes in the landscape – a junction, a steep hill, a wet bend. The regular group knows each other's strengths and weaknesses and positions on the road change accordingly. Our strongest climber is a tall, lean rider. On the steepest slopes of the North Downs we create gaps for him to dart through, then let his titanium frame disappear into the darkness.

Often there is a comfortable silence: riding together is enough. The shared sounds of breathing, whirring freewheels, click-click of gear changes.

After about half an hour our legs have loosened up, and we've settled into this morning's riding conditions. The roads are damp. The air, though not cold, is laden with a fine mist. The dawn is little more than a streak of light grey behind the clouds. At Keston the pavement ends. Not that we're riding on the pavement, but this moment is significant because I think of it as a practical definition of where the city ends. The authorities are saying, beyond this point we do not expect you to walk alongside roads. You're off our patch now, good luck.

Crudely, we can divide the whole of the landscape into three zones – city, suburbs, country. It's tricky to define why city is different to suburbs: both have the same jumble of contents, both are defined by human presence and activity, and in roadside terms the cyclist has the same view of life whether he is in Lambeth or Bromley. But we intuitively understand the differences. In the suburbs there is a greater emphasis on housing, and more of a sense of space. While the city's structures are forced upwards, the suburbs sprawl across the land. Between the suburbs and the country there is a more marked difference. One moment the cyclist is moving past pavement and houses, the next it's a hedge and fields. From human living space to horse living space.

Every cyclist who likes to escape the city, who heads for green space, will have two or three routes out of town, and on every route he will have a marker for the point where city ends and country begins. Often it's the start of hedges and fields, but it may be more oblique than that. It may just be a quiet stretch of road, a view of the hills, or simply the point at which the rider can relax, can breathe a little deeper. I accept that perhaps not every cyclist is as obsessed with topography as I am, and may not consciously consider such things, but I do believe that landscape works on all of us, massages our brains, even if we don't register it consciously.

It's easy to get morose about having to ride through the suburbs. Visually there is little enticing about row after row of 1930s houses, parades of shops, car dealerships, warehouses, light industrial estates. On my own route through Bromley there is a section of road that could be very fast and enjoyable if only there wasn't always a long queue of traffic there every Saturday and Sunday morning. The reason for the queue? Householders taking rubbish to the tip; could there be a more suburban way to spend your weekends?

Lazy thinking is tempting, like getting a takeaway on a Friday night. It's tiring, thinking like a novelist all the time. So let's be lazy for a while and go with the well-trodden perception of suburbia as dull, a place of comfort for the prematurely old, and for the young a place to escape from. I like to kid myself that my own part of South London is more city than suburb, but this is a purely arbitrary judgement based on my own wishful thinking. Probably, for someone living in Bermondsey, my area is considered suburban and deadly dull. OK for raising children, once you get to that stage of life.

Some of my neighbours are fond of saying, in a rather smug way, 'It's like a village round here'. By which they mean that people talk to each other on the street, pop in and out of each other's houses clutching bottles of Prosecco, bump into each other at the school gates and in the supermarket and at the children's ballet classes.

My neighbourhood is nothing like a village. Because, among all its urban diversity, those with similar backgrounds and outlooks seek each other out. The toddlers bring their parents together with other parents but that's only half the job. There is then a very subtle, but extremely rigorous filtering process, so that friendships are based on shared tastes. Perfectly natural, and I'm sure the same thing happens in every city around the world. But their reference to an archetypal English village is telling. For this way of living, the world of H. J. Massingham, the world of Hambleden, and of Watlington, remains something we wish to return to.

Perhaps that explains why, when we ride out of the city, we're so keen to get from city to country. The zone between is just annoying.

When Edward Thomas cycled from London to Gloucestershire in 1913, the journey that formed the basis for his book *In Pursuit of Spring*, he passed through Morden and Crystal Palace, and wasn't very impressed.

'It is so easy to make this flat land sordid. The roads, hedges and fences on it have hardly a reason for being anything but straight. More and more the kind of estate disappears that might preserve trees and various wasteful and pretty things: it is replaced by small villas and market gardens. If any waste be left under the new order, it will be used for conspicuously depositing rubbish. Little or no wildness of form or arrangement can survive, and with no wildness a landscape cannot be beautiful. Barbed wire and ugly and cruel fences, used against the large and irresponsible population of townsmen, add to the charmless artificiality. It was a relief to see a boy stealing up one of the hedges, looking for birds' nests. And then close up against this eager agriculture and its barbed wires are the hotels, inns, teashops, and cottages with ginger beer for the townsman who is looking for country of a more easygoing nature. This was inhospitable.'

Oh, the sneering! The derision of 'ginger beer for the townsman who is looking for country of a more easygoing nature'. Thomas was one of our finest poets of the English landscape, an oft-troubled man who loved to be alone in the countryside, and wrought lasting art from those times. His predecessor, at least the writer he greatly admired, was Richard Jefferies, the Wiltshire naturalist who in 1877, at the age of 28 and with a young family, went to live in Surbiton, that bastion of middle-class suburbia. There he wrote an influential book on the way nature was forced within London to improvise.

Since Thomas, landscape writing has ebbed and flowed; recently it has seen a major resurgence. Mostly it has lost its snobbishness towards the suburban, the liminal, in part because modern writers and artists have investigated and celebrated such places. This new focus on edgelands, as they have been called, has given nature writing its critical update. And yet, for all the hundreds, possibly thousands, of pages I have read about the British countryside, none of it has stuck in my head the way one passage has from Alain de Botton's book about Marcel Proust.

In *How Proust Can Change Your Life*, de Botton relates that one of Proust's favourite publications was the train timetable for the line from Paris St-Lazare to Le Havre. Proust would read the lists of stations on each branch line and imagine the people getting on and off the train at each, the houses they were headed to, their lives. Proust, de Botton says, was capable of immense imaginative empathy, and this was at the heart of his writing.

I was shocked and deeply impressed by this anecdote about Proust. Whether or not it's true – and I have no reason to believe it's not – it says a great deal about the job of a writer. That is, to imagine himself into the lives of others, then convey those lives into stories. Proust was concerned here with place and landscape, but only in the sense that it was a specific location at a specific time, and it therefore framed any potential story that might come from his timetable musings. More important, much more important, were the lives of the people living in these places. In books, character should come before everything else.

I identify as a novelist. A failed novelist, because I have yet to publish a novel, but a novelist all the same.

My most recent novel expired because there was something irretrievably wrong with its structure. I put it through months of rewriting treatments but no amount of cosmetic surgery could hide the fact that its very bone structure was flawed. I threw it, and fiction aside, to focus on cycling journalism and a non-fiction book about cyclo-cross. I stopped reading fiction, I stopped reading the reviews of the latest novels. And through this process I discovered the thing I'd been missing: empathy. It feels a little shameful for a man in his early 40s to say he's never felt empathy before. But what I mean is that I'd never realised just how deeply a novelist must look at the people around him. I had experienced empathy, of course, but never before had I really put *effort* into it. I'd thought that ideas were enough, when combined with an interesting landscape and some recognisable characters. I was on Proust's train, but I was looking at the places, not the people. For all those years I was too reliant on place, too scared of people and their messy lives, too shy to strip back all the layers of psychology and emotion and social interaction.

By the time my last novel was dying, I was living in London. Still riding, though I hated the way I was forced to ride through suburbs for six miles before I saw a field, and the narrow choice of rides thereafter. The city felt, at first, designed to discourage cycling. But then I began to commute to work and I got a new sense of the city. I saw the people getting off the train, not the place. For all its demands, London feels like a place where the future lies, where society cuts its teeth on new ideas. You don't get that feeling in Tring or Watlington. And there is something about the intensity of living in London that makes you confront the realities of human life. Everywhere you look, there are stories.

On this dark February morning we are seeking escape from the city, even if only for two hours, because we all need to be home and showered by 10, ready for children's swimming lessons, church services, family days out. In those two hours we can do little more than climb the long slope to the top of the ridge of North Downs hills that runs like a protective rim around the south-east of London, holding the M25 out, drop down the precariously steep scarp slopes, almost all shrouded in trees, then turn immediately and ride back up. We will see the sun rising over the Weald, but will turn our backs on that invitingly dense landscape.

For a few minutes we ride along the Pilgrim's Way, a sinew of tarmac that runs along the foot of the North Downs and is treasured by South London cyclists. Here, the Way runs parallel to the dull roar of the M25, but near the ancient church of St Botolph's, just outside Sevenoaks, the Way leaps over the motorway and continues its path to Canterbury. Like the Icknield Way in Tring, this section of road that we cyclists so enjoy is only a small part of a much longer and more diffuse route. The Pilgrim's Way starts in Winchester and crosses the Hampshire Downs and the Surrey Hills before skirting the North Downs and then dipping into Kent.

When Edward Thomas eulogised this Way, in *Spring on the Pilgrim's Way*, a chapter from *The South Country*, published in 1906, he delighted in the varied landscape that the path passed across. From farm lowlands and meadows to high open hills, then plunging deep into woods and hollows. Today the path is the same combination of footpath, track and country lane it was then, and while roads and houses have sprouted around it, one can still sense the ghosts of its countless travellers.

Sips of cold energy drink, fiddling with zips to keep out cold, damp air, beginning to feel in tune with the road, being aware of the shapes I'm pedalling. *Souplesse* marks you out as a racer, even if you're producing a meagre amount of power. On the long gradual climb of Beddlestead Lane, a quiet road that wends between meadows and could be located in the Belgian Ardennes, a favourite of London cyclists heading south, I tell myself to stay at the back of the group with the slowest rider, to ride humbly. I just can't do it. Evidently I am still competitive in nature. I'm not the fittest in this group but I want to be at the front, testing myself against the others. A clumsy pride perhaps, borne of my own nostalgia for racing. *I used to be good*, I want to tell the others. *I could have blitzed up here on the big ring.* But who cares about that now? I don't want to be one of those men who lives on the memories of what he did aged 18, nor do I want to forget what cycling has meant to me. There are times when I want to race again, to feel that full-blooded visceral thrill of being in the peloton, of competition that is openly declared, rather than this none-too-subtle showing of strength in what should just be a friendly Sunday morning spin.

Perhaps that is part of the fate of growing older, into middle-age, that competition has to become more muted, more nuanced. Material success at 18 is about how much cash you have in your pocket and how new your trainers are. At 40, it's about house prices. At 18, romantic success could be the number of partners you've had, or whether you've secured a partner above your own league. By 40, success could be construed as being happy in your relationship. 'Happy' being an infinitely more complex state to define than whether your girlfriend is at least as attractive as you are.

If, by 40, you consider yourself to be a happy man, that's an enviable position to be in. If, by 40, you have learned to open your eyes and try to see something of how the world connects, and then turn those observations into art, whatever its quality, that makes you a fortunate man. And if, by 40, you have learned the power of empathy, that briefly imagining yourself into someone else's skin can make you feel alive in your own, then you have a skill that will break and mend your heart many times over. Outwardly, society places no value on these things, and it is very difficult to communicate them to your friends and peers without looking like a smug bastard. Or even a bit weird.

The term 'mid-life crisis' is generally scoffed at. Either by those who are too young to understand it, or by those who can look back at their own with some humour. And mid-life crises have been given a bad name by their association with sports cars, illicit love affairs and exercise machines rusting in the garage. I have witnessed at close quarters one particular mid-life crisis that featured all three, and it wasn't pretty. Some men (and it does seem to be men who indulge in mid-life crises) manage to channel their fear of death into something more productive and benign; one friend became obsessed with his lawn for several months, lavishing so much attention on it that his wife became jealous, which must have been disorienting for her because it's easy to conceive how to be jealous of another woman, but a patch of grass is altogether different.

The collapse of my novel happened just before I turned 40. Serendipitous. My mid-life crisis manifested itself as a switch between literary genres. To the external viewer, that is to say everyone else, the fact that I had written fiction and was now going to try some non-fiction probably didn't seem ground-shaking. To me, having obsessed over fiction for almost 20 years, it was bold, scary, exciting and disappointing. This last adjective applies because I felt like a failure: I'd failed in my stated aim to publish a novel and rather than battering onwards against the headwind, I'd turned round to enjoy the tailwind. Non-fiction was easier, was something of a cop-out. It was the sunlit, smoothly surfaced lane dropping through the landscape. Of course, I soon discovered this view to be false, that no descent comes without a corresponding ascent, and in non-fiction some of the climbs can make your wheels feel like they are made of lead.

Still the sense of failure persisted. I'd failed at cycling because I wanted to turn professional but had got nowhere near. I'd failed at writing because I wanted to win the Booker Prize but hadn't even got into print. What do two negatives make? A positive. Writing about cycling came relatively easily, I enjoyed it, got paid and got into print – magazines, then a book. I loved cycling and I'd learned the craft of writing, and putting them together seemed to work.

By failing at these two things, my two biggest passions, then putting them together, I'd somehow made myself happy.

The fast roll back into Bromley, some moments of gleeful cornering, half-sprinting for speed cameras, laughing and piss-taking. Any snatches of conversation tend not to be about children. Just two hours, enjoy every minute.

Salisbury Plain

Snoring from the back. Thank God. A quick check in the mirror confirms that both children are indeed asleep, their perfect little faces pointed slightly upwards, mouths agape. Only a few minutes ago we were having the same question and answer session we have on every long road journey: is this a motorway or an A-road? How many minutes until we're there? Is it a long motorway? What's a junction?

It's astounding how quickly they can go from lively interrogation to unconsciousness. But then my answers were deliberately boring. Try imagining yourself into the mind of a seven-year-old, learning for the first time all those strange things we think utterly mundane. Road furniture, how bricks work, sarcasm, why people sometimes lie. Small wonder we parents have to keep repeating ourselves.

Sleep was part of the plan, so I'm relieved. It's seven o'clock on a Friday evening and we're heading south-west on the M3, into a promisingly vibrant sunset. Whenever we do this journey, a few times a year, we try to leave just before the children's bedtime so the car rocks them to sleep, and when we arrive at our destination we can transfer them straight into their makeshift beds. It doesn't always work out that way, but it's generally a pretty good system.

My wife is asleep too, so I've only got Radio 4 for company, and a bag of fruit pastilles to chew on. Swooping away from the motorway, I take the A303 and instantly feel better. This is the point at which I feel London receding, the point at which we move into a calmer, more open space. Not many roads have a paperback biography *and* a television series. The A303 does. Its fame, and the affection so many hold for it, is based on its role in ferrying families to their holidays in the West Country. My parents took us on the M4 because it was much faster from where we lived, but just as my sister and I woke up to find ourselves passing Bristol City Docks, many other children woke to find themselves deep in the rolling Somerset hills.

Before then, however, are the Hampshire North Downs and Salisbury Plain. Three lanes become two, become one. The road climbs and falls, carves a path around towns like Andover and Basingstoke. In the dusk-dimmed land to either side of the road there is fertile farmland, ancient sites, half-asleep villages, lanes that will soon be busy with night creatures. Towards the end of my journey the structure of Stonehenge is just about visible against the blue-black sky. I simply peer forward and press the accelerator.

Stonehenge is a place I'm not sure how I feel about; when I first visited, you were allowed to wander between the stones, now visitors are kept so far back they may as well be in a car passing along the nearby road, as I am. I cast a glance at the stones, pay a moment's silent respect, and try not to think about *Spinal Tap*.

Soon after, the road drops into a deep valley and I know we are almost at journey's end. Turn off at the village of Wylye, and abruptly we've switched from fast dual carriageway to narrow lanes lined with thatched cottages. Having come from London, the quietness and the darkness is a shock. In London at this time life is still being lived on the streets, in shops and cafés and bars. Here, my prejudices have everyone curled up on the sofa, watching *Midsomer Murders*.

A road out of the village takes me across a level crossing and up a steep hill. Change down, foot to the floor, headlights flick onto full beam, catching rabbits plunging into the hedgerow. The hill goes on and on, breaking out of woods and crossing exposed fields, a huge star-filled sky embracing the land. Tomorrow morning, I will ride down here on my bike. Tomorrow morning, I fly.

Sarah and Daniel live in a farmhouse just over the top of this hill. *Farmhouse* is an accurate description, Daniel being a farmer, but the building confounds any stereotypes of what a farmhouse should look like. A modern red-brick three-bedroom house, built only 15 years ago, it occupies a position that is half-pastoral and half-industrial. From the front door and windows, the view is dominated by a huge steel shed that used to be a home for dairy cows but now is used mainly for storing grain and machinery. From the back windows, beyond the modest garden strewn with children's toys, there are fields and woods as far as one can see. The lane to get here is down there somewhere, almost buried. In every direction the land is owned by Daniel's family farm.

We have that kind of friendship with Sarah and Daniel that we can let ourselves in, say hello and plonk ourselves down on the sofa, without them even getting up. I like this. To feel this comfortable in someone else's home is a wonderfully precious thing.

Morning starts with noise elsewhere in the house. The noise of six children getting reacquainted with each other. Sarah and Daniel have two girls and twin boys. The boys are close in age to my youngest, my son. The second girl is a year older than my daughter. They fall as easily back into each other's company as us grown-ups. I pull on my cycling shorts, here is my opportunity.

Half an hour later, I'm pulling my bike out of their shed. My pockets are loaded with tools, money and stolen chunks of Easter egg (the kids get so many they don't notice when one gets attacked by their father), my two bottles full of pinkish energy drink, and my high-pressure tyres ping away loose gravel chips as I ride tentatively past the dairy shed and the grassy enclosure that awaits this year's delivery of lambs. For a few years now Sarah has been taking orphaned lambs from the neighbouring sheep farmer, caring for them in this meadow in front of her house, and then sending them to the abattoir just before Christmas. Sometimes we buy one of the lambs, watch its progress through the year, and come to collect it in a set of large freezer bags in the winter. I'm not evangelical about food provenance, but I am proud that my children understand the realities of what they are eating, the sacrifices involved, and something of the process.

Bump off the farm track and onto the semi-submerged lane, and away. A cold mist hangs low over the fields. The verges are heavy with dew. Small creatures – voles? – scurry away on my approach. In the undulating field between the lane and Sarah's back garden a hare stops and assesses this new movement in his world, then darts away. I'm reminded that as well as being an ancient symbol of Easter, there are folk tales of hares being witches in disguise. When I told that one to Daniel he replied by saying that witches on his land would probably cause less trouble. Modern farming methods have caused a decline in the numbers of hares in rural Britain over the last 50 years. If they're not shot by farmers, the average British hare has to run from poachers, foxes and buzzards. No wonder this one was jumpy.

My rather romantic view of farming comes, naturally, from books. My earliest years in Watlington are distant, yet I retain the memories of exploring the surrounding fields and woods, of Bonfire Night at Manor Farm in nearby Cuxham, where you could sit on bales of hay and eat toffee apples while the fire climbed to the stars, and of Christmas Eve when all the children would pile into a trailer to be pulled by a tractor to St Leonard's Church. And if my life has moved away from such scenes, to that of a city dweller, I have fuelled my personal nostalgia with a more literary type; for example, the work of farmer-writer Adrian Bell, who lived and worked in Suffolk for much of his life and produced some 25 books. In memoirs like *Men and the Fields* and *Apple Acre*, Bell uses his beautifully understated yet lyrical prose to describe his work on the farm and life in the tiny hamlet around him. This is a world sometimes described as 'vanished' but the minutiae of family life that he lovingly captures, and the more profound relationship with the land, aren't much changed.

Daniel may have expensive technology to make his work easier, and more precise, but the application of it still depends on the rhythm of seasons. Activity, yields, income, all hinge on the weather.

Into the wood at the top of the hill, its floor of bluebells looking icy and fragile. And then out into the open. The road curves over the hill like a cartoon, nothing but a pencil stroke across the green. And it carries me, faster and faster, with the patchwork farmland of Salisbury Plain spread out to my left, to my right, dead ahead. Overhead there may be thin blue skies but down here the cold is penetrating. I'm wearing full-finger gloves, a neck-warmer, leg warmers and three layers on my body. As my eyes stream, despite my sunglasses, the bike is travelling so fast it demands my total attention.

At the bottom of the hill, having skipped over the railway level crossing, I stiffly manhandle the bike through a T-junction and begin pedalling to warm up mind, body and soul. This lane, running from Wylye to Wilton, a small market town on the outskirts of Salisbury, is one of the most beautiful few miles of riding I know. The road meanders alongside the River Wylye, bordered by fields and meadows, a couple of farms, tidy hamlets in which the houses are all built from the same yellow limestone. From time to time the road dips into a copse of ash and elder. Beside the river are gracefully relaxed willows. The road rises and falls a little, bends a little, has its fair share of holes and cracks. As I move silently through this scene I can look across the valley at the hills rising to the north, or I can pull faces at the cows watching me from beyond the fences.

I'm conscious that from the way I've just described this stretch of road it perhaps doesn't sound like the most beautiful section of road ever graced by my two wheels. Pleasant, yes, but the most beautiful?

Well, beauty is a complex thing. First, there is consistency. This road has never let me down; no freezing rain, no punctures, no angry drivers, no howling headwinds. Second, this valley gives me the sense of being more connected to the landscape than in other places. In part this is because I'm staying with Daniel, who owns and works much of this land, and that it sits within the wider expanses of the Plain, with all its ancient history. It is both a landscape of the ages and one of moments so fleeting they can hardly be grasped. Early one autumn morning I was riding along this road and caught a movement out of the corner of my eye. A barn owl was gliding alongside me, 15 feet away. For four seconds, at most, I watched its effortless flight, then it wheeled away out of sight.

The views I absorb as I ride are ever-changing, season by season, and while only brief and occasional, I enjoy the feeling that my presence is recurrent, that I am loyal in my own tiny way.

The links between cycle racing and agriculture are surprisingly strong. Many top professionals have come from farming backgrounds. The hardness of the farming life is said to form the kind of character you need to battle through Flanders in driving rain for 130 miles. The racing cyclist spends his days, whether training or racing, working on the land.

In *Velo*, Paul Fournel writes that the cyclist is akin to a peasant: 'There's something of the peasant in the pedaller. They share a taste for nature, submission to the elements, patience, thrift, perseverance, and the sense of acceleration.'

Yet the cyclist is different to the peasant, at least to the farmworker, in one regard: he stays free of the physical reality of the land. In her introduction to the Little Toller edition of Edward Thomas's *In Pursuit of Spring*, Alexandra Harris cites John Clare's poem for March in his *Shepherd's Calendar*, saying that it's a poem of 'stooping, splashing, chopping, leaping, striding, slinging, strewing, in which hands and feet are constantly moving through the "many weathers" of the season'.

If I return from my ride spattered with Wiltshire mud it's probably because a tractor has been on the road before me, shedding soil from its tyres. These days the impressively advanced machinery of the farm does the stooping and splashing, but it's Daniel or his brother at the wheel, using GPS to plan their drilling while listening to Radio 4.

Unobtrusively the lane slips into Wilton. I pass antiques shops and cafés, stately houses, and at the town centre traffic lights I turn right to climb up onto the Downs once more. It's a steady hill, mostly shaded by woods, and not too troubling. I know that there will be more climbing to come, so I measure my effort.

The descent is open and fast but it doesn't drop the same amount as I've just climbed. Instead the road hits another that runs up the Ebble Valley, gradually climbing towards Prescombe Down. This valley road is impossibly cute at times, with its glassy stream alongside, its neat cottages teetering on the hillside and its explosions of daffodils. This early on a Saturday there are a few people around, but mostly the houses are blank to my gaze. I let them drift by and wonder what lives are playing out within those honey-coloured walls, what quiet dramas, what secret passions.

Perhaps the saying shouldn't be that there is a novel in all of us, but that there is a novel about any of us. Some days I see stories everywhere I look; other days the lives of others seem utterly closed to me.

Sarah and Daniel's story might provide the framework for a good novel. They went to the village primary school together, then Sarah's parents moved the family away to Kent, where Sarah met my wife when they both had a Saturday job at their local Woolworth's. Sarah trained and worked as a nurse, and on a weekend trip back to Wiltshire she met some of her old classmates in the pub, including Daniel. As their relationship developed she moved back to Wiltshire to be with him, got married and had children.

Not wholly remarkable, as novel foundations go. Yet there is a built-in conflict to this situation. Daniel's farm is family-owned and has been for several generations. He is connected to this land in a way that it's hard for a non-farmer to conceive of. He will never leave this place. He will never leave the farm. The farm is an entity in its own right, its existence never questioned. This sense of permanence and commitment to something enduring is appealing to me, it's the same sense of commitment I have to writing. But it can also be restrictive, and for Sarah, a woman who had her own career in London, and has known other ways of living, there are sacrifices to living as a farmer's wife.

Extrapolate from this situation and there are some interesting dramatic themes – traditional versus modern modes of living, gender politics in modern rural life, the problems that can arise when family businesses are handed down over the generations.

And yet I will never write this novel. Not out of respect for Sarah and Daniel's privacy – I believe a writer should feel equipped to chase any subject, and has to have a sliver of ice in his heart to do so. No, I will not write this novel because I'm not sure my empathy can effectively pierce the inner life of a farmer. There are some things that I can identify with Daniel about, particularly the obsession with work that owning your own business can create. But the rhythm of his days, the minutiae of what he does, is so utterly different to my own life that I'm not sure I'd ever adequately understand that way of life. Not enough to be able to write a convincing character.

I might know the network of roads around here, but Daniel knows every field, track and barn in between. He knows the weather, the drainage of the land, the animals, the yields, the politics of local landowners.

Or, to return to the realisation I had after the trip to Cley Hill, I am essentially an urban animal. My soul is refreshed by the countryside, but I am no longer at home here. Perhaps, had my life taken some different turns, I might have lived in a place like this. But such thinking is pretty pointless. I love it here, but I'll no more move out here than Daniel will move to London.

This valley road sneaks up behind a row of big hills, but at some point you have to make the decision to turn and face one of them. Like the Blowing Stone Hill in Oxfordshire, these climbs are direct and deceptively brutal. Now that the mist has been burned off and spring sunshine is swimming in the secluded valley, I'm getting warm enough to start peeling off layers of clothing. *Drink up*, I remind myself, *dehydration isn't just for those balmy June days*.

My destination is the airfield at Compton Abbas, which has a café and a viewing area, where you can drink your tea and watch light aircraft make their far-fetched leaps into the great blue yonder. It's a spectacular spot, high on the steep-sided chalk hills of Cranborne Chase, with expansive views to the north, where the hills rise in lynchet steps; ancient strips cut into the hillsides created by ploughing strips along the hillsides.

Sometimes, on a weekend trip to the farm, I will head north, across the A303 and into these hills. The landscape there is just a little more open, and a little more empty than the pretty valleys around Wilton. Perhaps that's because the ground is higher and there are fewer rivers. One summer's morning, riding over the top of an exposed and silent hillside, there was a sudden roar away to my left and a tank came crunching out of a pit beside the road. I nearly fell off my bike. The tank's gun was pointing at me when it emerged, but quickly swivelled away, though I did have to slam my brakes on to allow the beast to charge across the road. I say 'allow' – there was never any likelihood of me stopping it. This is tank country. Ministry of Defence country. Salisbury Plain has the largest area of protected chalk grassland in the country, because of the huge swathes of land owned by the MoD. While armoured vehicles rumble across muddy tracks, orchids, wild thyme, butterflies, grasshoppers and bees all thrive.

Ride a few miles east and you will pass the secretive establishment at Porton Down, home of the government's research into chemical weapons. It's a place as secret and sinister as the Atomic Weapons Establishment, though it's never quite captured my imagination in the way AWE did, probably because very few of its buildings are visible from public roads. The land around Porton Down's top-secret research laboratories is undisturbed chalk grassland, and because it hasn't been ploughed or burned, there is a concentration of juniper bushes that support many types of insect.

There is a curious mix of people in the café at the Compton Abbas airfield – aeroplane enthusiasts, the families of those going up into the heavens, cyclists, walkers and quite often a gang of middle-aged bikers. Compared to the dull but also utterly incomprehensible business of getting passenger jets off the Gatwick runways, the operation here at Compton Abbas is much more contingent, much more excitingly human. The runway is grass and not entirely flat. The aeroplanes are surprisingly diverse in their size and style, but they are all small enough to remind me of the dinghies my father used to sail around the creeks of Cornwall. Delicate-looking but effective and robust, powered by simple technology, devoid of the computers that have come to dominate and confuse our existence. The moment when a microlight or vintage Tiger Moth leaves the ground always creates a little gasp, sometimes a cheer. Lifting yourself into the sky with a tiny engine in a fibreglass shell is an act of courage, levity, freedom.

From the café the road runs fast, slightly downhill, then drops over the edge of Win Green. This is one of those descents which, if taken correctly, can be done without touching the brakes. The bends are gentle but the road surface is scratchy. Flying at 50 miles per hour down here is exhilarating, but striking a hole could be very unpleasant indeed.

When I get back to the farmhouse the children are running loose in the garden, my wife and Sarah are having a coffee on the patio, and Daniel, naturally, is at work. Three hours of riding down here is harder than three hours back home, so I'm tired. A shower, tea and hearty snacks, a quick sit down and then the children draw me into their splendid chaos. This is happiness.

Back in London a few weeks later I secure a new commission – a feature about the End to End, Britain's longest journey, Land's End to John O'Groats. I've never ridden it, nor anything even close, and I have to persuade myself that it's valid for me to write about something of which I have no direct experience. Wearing my cycling journalist's *casquette* I can write about the experiences of others, yet to speculate more generally about the motives people have for long-distance adventures finds me in uncomfortable territory.

All I can say is that my idea of the perfect bicycle ride is about three hours, on rolling roads, a sunny day, perhaps a decent café to aim for. Is this a failure of adventure on my part? Yes, probably. Or to be more precise, is it the triumph of anxiety over exploration?

On a family holiday to the South of France a few years ago, I hired a road bike and set off one morning for a ride that looked, on my map at least, fairly simple. The first section proved to be so: a stunning spin along the coast as the sun climbed into the sky. Then I climbed too, over a small hill that took me inland and towards the range of bigger peaks looking down on the Côte d'Azur. As I descended into a small town, I punctured. No trouble; I had a spare tube, tyre levers and a pump. I changed the tube then told myself that if I could find a bike shop in the town I'd buy another tube so as to continue the ride. I found the shop, but it being Saturday, the shop was closed. After a bit of eye-rolling at the French idea of retail, I had to decide whether to carry on or turn back. This town was roughly a third of the way into the ride. *May as well carry on…*

What my map didn't convey was the nature of the road that would be taking me home. It began ascending through a housing estate then disappeared into the warm, sweet-smelling pine woods that proliferate that region. A stiff climb, but I wasn't unfit, and had been over worse earlier in the week. I kept going. Then the road surface began to crumble at the edges, great fissures opened up before me. I found myself weaving back and forth across the road to avoid losing my front wheel. Which is not all bad, because it takes one's mind away from the pain of climbing.

Five kilometres out of town the poor excuse for a tarmac surface gave up entirely and I found myself on a gravel track. At this point I began to consider turning back. I had no spare tube, my rear tyre was softer than I would usually have it, my mobile had no reception, and I hadn't seen a single other person since leaving the town. If I punctured up here, I would have to ride it flat, very slowly, back down to the town. Then what?

I carried on. Hardly a death-defying act of courage, I can sense you thinking, and you are indeed right. Yet for me, whose rides, and much more, are always controlled, always planned, it was an act of spontaneous adventure. I trusted fate not to push one of these little stones I was crunching over into my tyres. I didn't attempt to formulate a contingency plan, I just rode. Up and up the track looping across the hillside, the town and coastline becoming more hazy with every passing minute. I felt utterly alone. The cicadas buzzed their welcome. Little lizards darted across the road. Sheep and goats skipped and lurched through the trees above me. The climb seemed to go on forever, but of course eventually it flattened out, before dropping away. On the way down I came across a sheep with what looked like an injured leg, trying to limp along the track. I passed it carefully, wondering whether there was anything I could do to help. No, what could I do – strap it to my back? Around the next bend I found a shepherd, a girl of 20 or so, coaxing her flock along. I tried to explain in my *très mauvais* French that one of her team was off the back of the peloton with an injury. She smiled sadly and nodded.

Adventure calls for a lively sense of being alive in a world that isn't always benign. Adventure means being open but also defensive. The senses are dialled up, adrenaline will get you through. The explorer's imperative is to discover the landscape and most importantly to survive it. The act of surviving underlines what it means to be alive. I get that. Who can feel more alive than the rock climber who has cheated gravity and death, or the microlight pilot who has climbed higher than a hawk then brought his machine back to earth with only a gentle bump?

For me, though, cycling is not adventure. Cycling is about mapping the small worlds that are always around us, being receptive to their transformative qualities, tuning into their precise and delicate frequencies, connecting the constellations of meaning that every place contains.

Escape does not necessarily equate to adventure. And adventure does not necessarily equate to distance. The machismo of wilderness adventure is not for me. I have to consciously resist the pressure that exists in cycling culture to tick off experiences – the greatest climbs, the iconic routes, the 10 must-do events... Such rhetoric somehow makes the thing I love into capital. A life spent on two wheels shouldn't have to be about accumulating achievements as if they were wealth.

I may have failed at bike racing, I may have failed at writing fiction, but these three-hour journeys around my own landscape have helped to make me a happy man. That's not so bad, is it?

Loops

Books, I'll always return to books.

When I began thinking about this book, I did what I suspect many writers do at the same stage – I went into a book-buying frenzy. Soon there was a hefty pile of beautiful hardbacks on my desk. Many had green covers. Books about landscape, books about trees, books about paths, books about hedgerows. I told myself that I had to read these books before I committed a word to the page, and yet I was soon seized with a sense of inertia. You could also call it boredom. Much of what I was reading felt like escapism, and while there's nothing wrong with that in itself, it wasn't helping me think through what I wanted my own book to say.

Then, in a small but significant act of rebellion, I picked from my bookshelves a slender volume I'd been given by my wife many years before but had never got round to reading. Published by the Princeton Architectural Press, the book was called *Geography of Home* by Akiko Busch.

Devoting each chapter to a different room in the house, Busch explores the meanings of the humble spaces where we live and how our emotional life resonates through them. After reading so many sentences about sleeping out in Iron Age barrows, stalking otters at dawn and the way a shaft of sunlight catches Lakeland granite, it was a relief to read about why people work at the kitchen table and our collective reluctance to abolish the utterly pointless dining room. It was literally like coming home. I followed up with more books on architecture and interiors.

Does this mean I'm not really the outdoors sort? That in writing a book about landscape and cycling I've committed an act of fraud? I don't think so, for exploration and comfort go hand in hand. Who doesn't, after being blasted by wind and sun, after climbing over hills and plunging back to the valley floor, enjoy coming home to buttered toast and endless cups of tea?

A few years ago I read a book called *Into the Wild* by Jon Krakauer. You may have read it too, or seen the film adaptation. Something of a modern classic, it investigates the death and life of Chris McCandless in Alaska, in 1992. McCandless was 24 when he walked alone into the Alaskan wilderness. Four months later, his emaciated body was found in an old abandoned bus, where he'd set up camp. Krakauer's book attempts to unravel the tragedy, to explain how he died, the physical causes, and why he died, the psychology of McCandless' actions.

The book is a vivid portrait of an idealistic, intelligent and rebellious young man who longs for adventure. McCandless seems not to have the same mechanisms of fear and self-limiting that most of us do. He was always on the move, traversing America like Jack Kerouac, except Kerouac usually travelled with friends, stayed with acquaintances on both coastlines, and travelled well-trodden routes. McCandless was a true loner, few people got close to him. He loved nature and literature, hated modern consumerist life. Before his ill-fated venture into the brutal Alaskan wilderness around Mount McKinley, McCandless gave away all his possessions and money. The fact that he went into such an unforgiving landscape with inadequate clothing and equipment, and only a bag of rice, leads to the question of whether he wanted to die out there. Krakauer, naturally, cannot definitively answer this question. He can only draw a portrait of McCandless and leave the reader to draw their own conclusions.

I finished the book feeling distinctly uncomfortable – I didn't know how to react. Chris McCandless baffled me. If I'd started the story thinking that I might admire his adventurous nature, his lack of fear, I soon realised that my principal feeling towards him was anger. What about all the people he'd left behind, the family who loved him? Perhaps he was academically brilliant, but his practical stupidity had cost him his life, and condemned his family to grief. Or was that what he wanted? Was his quest for a new kind of experience, raw and transcendent, to use Krakauer's words, a noble one, and death was part of the deal? Was I simply too conservative and safe to understand?

Part of the reason the book cut through me as it did is that McCandless died in the same year that I went to university: 1992, when I gave up bike racing, went partying, left home for Norwich. Had I known of the story at that time, would my reaction have been any different?

When I was 18 the horizon was everything. I wanted to know what lay beyond it. And yet my own adventures were modest. Moving in an uncompromising straight line, always forward, away from home, never interested me. Perhaps I've been fortunate in having nothing I wish to escape from, for surely that is one of the primary forces that propel adventurers out of the front door?

I think if I had have known about McCandless in 1992 I would have felt more admiration for his spirit of adventure. But if I'd abandoned university, packed a bag and headed for Reading bus station, my fate would likely have been similar to that of Richard Jefferies, the naturalist, author, and father of the Ridgeway Path. Aged 16 and hungry for travel, Jefferies and an older cousin hatched a plan to walk to Russia. They managed to get as far as France, found their language skills insufficient, and quickly returned to England. After that he spent his life examining with forensic intensity the Wiltshire landscape he grew up in.

I'm interested, it seems, in loops. Head out, then return. On the bike, on foot, in stories. No need to go far, just keep your eyes open. Our lives are full of loops. I sit here at my desk and look at a picture of my children. My daughter wants to be a writer. One of the aspects of my son's personality I love is that he is so similar to my wife. Tomorrow we go on holiday – always a good thing to do after the last page – and we'll sit on the same beach my parents took me to 40 years ago. Occasionally I go back to Watlington and stand at the top of the white mark, gazing down at the village where I grew up. Sentimental, perhaps, but then I watch a red kite circling overhead and I think that freedom doesn't mean escape, it can come from thinking and watching. And from coming home.

Author's Note

Throughout this book there are passages when I refer to 'the cyclist' – a kind of abstract being beamed down from space, clothed in Lycra and ready to hurtle through sleepy English villages. In these passages I have referred to this cyclist as 'he'. Of course a cyclist can be 'he' or 'she'. I have chosen to use 'he' simply because I am a man and this book is written from my perspective, based on my experiences. Perhaps in the future there will come a time when the reader, at the point of purchase, can select the gender of abstract pronouns in the text, but I don't think we're quite there yet.

I owe a debt of gratitude to all the people who have assisted me with this book, in particular my editors, Charlotte Atyeo and Charlotte Croft, and my agent, Ben Clark of Lucas Alexander Whitley Ltd. Many conversations, planned or spontaneous, pointed me down scenic narrative lanes. For all those who saw my eyes drifting away in reverie, my sincere thanks and apologies. Thank you to the Society of Authors, whose bursary helped me carve out some time to think and write.

This book was mainly written in the snug surroundings of the National Theatre's lobby, on London's South Bank. Much of my momentum, and any brief moments of lucidity, I owe to their wonderful coffee. Finally, thank you to my family for all those hours I've spent escaping on my bike, and into my notebook.

Select Bibliography

Barthes, Roland, *Mythologies* (New York: Hill and Wang, 2012)
Bell, Adrian, *Apple Acre* (Dorset: Little Toller, 2012)
Bell, Adrian, *Men and the Fields* (Dorset: Little Toller, 2009)
Blann, Michael, *Mountains: Epic Cycling Climbs* (London: Thames and Hudson, 2016)
Booker, Christopher, The Seven Basic Plots: Why We Tell Stories (London: Continuum, 2005)
Busch, Akiko, *Geography of Home* (New York: Princeton Architectural Press, 1999)
Chabon, Michael, *Wonder Boys* (London: Fourth Estate, 1995)
Chambers, Emma (ed.), *Paul Nash* (London: Tate, 2016)
Cheever, John, *Collected Stories and Other Writings* (New York: The Library of America, 2009)
Cheever, John, *The Wapshot Chronicle* (London: Vintage Classics, 1998)
Clifford, Sue and King, Angela, *England in Particular* (London: Hodder & Stoughton, 2006)
Cowper Powys, John, *Wolf Solent* (London: Penguin Classics, 2000)
Dauncey, Hugh and Hare, Geoff (eds.), *The Tour de France, 1903–2003* (London: Frank Cass, 2003)
Day, Jon, *Cyclogeography: Journeys of a London Bicycle Courier* (London: Notting Hill, 2015)

De Botton, Alain, *How Proust Can Change Your Life* (London: Picador, 1997)
Fisher, Mark, *Ghosts of my Life* (London: Zero Books, 2013)
Fournel, Paul, *Velo* (London: Rouleur, 2012)
Hughes, Ted, *Poetry in the Making: A Handbook for Writing and Teaching* (London: Faber, 2008)
Jamie, Kathleen, *Findings* (London: Sort Of, 2005)
Jefferies, Richard, *Story of My Heart: My Autobiography* (London: CreateSpace, 2013)
Jefferies, Richard, *The gamekeeper at home: sketches of natural history and rural life* (London: CreateSpace, 2017)
Jefferies, Richard, *Wildlife in a Southern County* (Dorset: Little Toller Books, 2011)
Krabbe, Tim, *The Rider* (London: Bloomsbury, 2002)
Krakauer, Jon, *Into the Wild* (London: Pan, 2011)
Leonard, Max, *Higher Calling* (London: Yellow Jersey Press, 2017)
Macdonald, Helen, *H Is for Hawk* (London: Jonathan Cape, 2014)
Macfarlane, Robert, *The Old Ways: A Journey on Foot* (London: Penguin, 2013)
Matless, David, *Landscape and Englishness* (London: Reaktion, 1998)
Minshull, Duncan (ed.), *The Vintage Book of Walking* (London: Vintage, 2000)
Papadimitriou, Nick, *Scarp* (London: Sceptre, 2012)
Pavord, Anna, *Landskipping* (London: Bloomsbury, 2016)
Scovell, Adam, *Folk Horror* (London: Auteur, 2017)
Seaton, Matt, *The Escape Artist* (London: Fourth Estate, 2002)
Solnit, Rebecca, *Wanderlust* (London: Granta, 2014)
Tanizaki, Junichiro, *In Praise of Shadows* (London: Vintage, 2001)
Thomas, Edward, *In Pursuit of Spring* (Dorset: Little Toller, 2016)
Thomas, Edward, *One Green Field* (London: Penguin, 2009)
Thomas, Edward, *The South Country* (Dorset: Little Toller, 2009)

Permissions

The author acknowledges the following permissions that were granted to reproduce extracts in this book:

Page 88: Extract from 'Meeting One's Madness' in *The Paris Review*, Megan Mayhew Bergman, November 2016, reproduced by kind permission of the author

Page 98: Extract from *The Rider*, Tim Krabbe, translator Sam Garrett © 2016 Bloomsbury Publishing Plc

Page 192: Extract from *Mountains: Epic Cycling Climbs* © 2016 Michael Blann, reproduced by kind permission of Thames & Hudson Ltd

Page 206: Extract from *Mountains of the Mind*, Robert Macfarlane © 2008, reproduced by kind permission of Granta

Page 209: Extract from *The Tour de France 1903–2003*, Philippe Gaboriau, Hugh Dauncey and Geoff Hare (eds) © 2003, reproduced by kind permission of the editor

Page 214: Extract from 'Need for the Bike', *Velo*, Paul Fournel © 2012, reproduced by kind permission of University of Nebraska Press

Page 227: Extract from *In Pursuit of Spring*, Edward Thomas © 2016, reproduced by kind permission of Little Toller Books